OH LA.
SEXY THI'
FUN
HAVE
HUGS
Anton
Dickson

Anton Dickson

CHRONICLES OF A LONDON CUMPIG

erotic memoirs
Volume I

ATELIER A-Z

A special thanks to producer / director PAUL MORRIS of Treasure Island Media (TIM) for giving me the opportunity to write this online blog, and to share it with his readers over the last year and a half. This is my personal little interpretation of what man on man sex can all be about...

Also a personal thanks to close friend and Director Liam Cole of TIM, for providing inspiration and guidance over the last few years, and for always being there to help me question the established ways of thinking.

ATELIER A-Z BOOKS
Published by atelier a-z
Stockholm, Sweden / London, UK
www.atelier-az.org

First online publication in US 2012-13 for Treasure Island Media
www.treasureislandblog.com/anton-dickson
First published in print in Great Britain in 2013

Cover Illustration by Liam Cole (2013)

ISBN: 978-91-87617-00-3 (pbk)
ISBN: 978-91-87617-01-0 (e-book)
ISBN: 978-91-87617-02-7 (hc)

"Sex is like eating, it's a physical need, that desires and requires variety. Why would I eat cereal for breakfast, lunch and dinner, or only have steak all day long?"

Anton Dickson

WEEK I

MEET Anton Dickson

My name is Anton Dickson. Some of you might know me from Liam Cole's films: In the Flesh, Full Tilt, Wild Breed, Pounded, Slammed, Overload and Outlaws etc, for Treasure Island Media, where these Chronicles were first published on-line. Or from my earlier 'safe sex' porn work.

I'm from Sweden, with Croatian/Serbian origin. I lived three years in France but the last fifteen years I've been based in London, enjoying all these horny Brit lads. It's been quite amazing giving them my big uncut Eastern European cock as often as I can manage. When not fucking my way through the UK, I work as an architect and photographer. I'm also a retired classical ballet dancer.

Now that you know about me, let me tell you what a horny day I had the other day. I was working in the architect office, looking out through the dirty window (feeling generally bored), when I got this text message to my phone:
"I'm downstairs i n the pub under your job, do you want a mouthful?" Wow, who am I to resist a massive load from a horny teen walking past the area? Naturally, I agreed to meet him in the pub toilet straight away, made an excuse to my boss, and popped down to the pub, where I eagerly swallowed the horny 19 year old's massive 8 inch uncut cock. He came so much I couldn't help but gag. Well zipped up, the boy left, and I went back to work.

Little did I know that I would get another text on Grindr an hour later: "I'm HORNY, can I suck your cock?" Seeing as I hadn't cum with the first lad, I said sure! I thought it would look a bit suspicious of me going to the pub toilet again, though, so I asked if he could come to my office toilets. When he arrived, he wasted no time getting to his knees. I was already so horny from my earlier adventure, the precum was flowing freely. A few minutes later, I came a massive load in his eager mouth. He kissed me after, so I got a good taste of it myself, yummy. Wiping my beard and letting the boy out of the toilet, I made my way back to my office desk. I already started liking this day a lot. Little did I know that more was to follow. After work, I arrived back at my flat, it had been raining so I was soaked. Remembering my husband was not going to be home for a couple of months, I thought why not log on to Gayromeo to see who was about? I could always film some of my arty porn clips of me sucking boys off, if nothing else. (The KUK-series, for web-links to videos and photos etc see last pages.)

Almost instantly I started getting messages of eager guys wanting to pop over. I never realized how many local hotties there were around me, so I invited one over. My first adventure, a horny, big dicked ginger boy, came quickly in my mouth. Tasty but, as it was a bit too quick for me to properly enjoy, I invited another one over.

This guy was a very handsome German dancer who had recently come out, so everything was new to him. Being a good mentor, I eased him in so he could really appreciate what he was getting himself into. He was so turned on he came two times, once while I was fucking him hard!

After he left, I posted on my Facebook, "5 a day keeps the doctor away," to which a clever little guy commented, "Only 5, its only 9.30pm you surely have time for one more." Just as I was about to respond, there was a knock at my door. I opened it and in came a guy, whom I'd forgot I'd made an appointment with the week before. I guess 6 a day keeps the doctor away...

Oh and I wish I could say its all exaggerated fiction, but unfortunately, or luckily (depending on your standpoint) it's all true hehe.

Hugs
Anton

Readers online comments:

I - I want free porn

II - These daily sex adventures are so ridiculously hot to read about. I want to be one of these boys!

III - I would like nothing more than to receive a good pounding from Anton especially since he's visiting L.A. Hit me up nigga'!

IV - "Sorry, this video does not exist"? Is the link broken?

V - Yeah the link was too naughty for them to handle lol, it was banned, hehe u should be able to find it on gaytube/x-tube though, just type in Anton Dickson, Hugs a

VI - Hit me up if you are ever in LA!

WEEK II

NAUGHTY

Hi again, guys! Another week, another lot of naughty adventures in my little corner of the world - this week mostly was the joys of Treasure Island Media, as I've been shooting a few really horny scenes for Liam Cole. The first scene was with awesome hot bottom lad Carl Jacobs, who we haven't seen since he did a horny scene with TIM in Liam's "Bad Influence." It was steamy hot from the moment I entered the bedroom, rimming and fucking him good, and making him gag on my fat cock, till I shot a load up his horny little butthole.

Next scene was a few days after, when I got to fuck a new recruit to the TIM stable, an awesome hot French guy I found for TIM (I don't even know his porn name yet, he's that fresh to the 'market', hehe). He was a horny muscle guy with a gorgeous bum to eat out and finger, and he took my fist as well - which of course made me even harder and hornier, making me slap my rock hard meat up his horny bumhole.

I also got to do a fantastic horny scene with the same bottom lad and awesome top/versatile lad Luke Pacoe, who has a massive knob. It was truly amazing, this fucking horny threesome scene with us pinning the French lad from both ends till we both shot up his bumhole, after double fucking him and fisting him till he was gagging for more.

But, being my usual self, that wasn't enough to satisfy my huge sexual appetite. So the evening after the first shoot, I had a horny young Asian boy over. Barebacking his smooth boy-hole and watching him gag on my fat cock was very satisfying, I have to say - I loved watching him lick my balls and suck my floppy cock even after I dumped two loads up him, while I was watching telly over his horny bumhole and fingering him enough to make him moan.

The sun has been out as well recently here in London, which brings out all the t-shirt clad lads on the lawns. On my way home through the park, I locked eyes with a local Arabic hotty and, as a true professional, I enticed him to come into the park toilets (with one look, not too obvious but not too subtle either, hehe), where I went into a cubicle and he joined me. He went down to his knees straight away and started sucking me. The piss stench in the toilets were strong, making me even hornier.

When I was getting really close, I pulled him up and pulled down his shorts and shot my load in his tight hairy hole - he was moaning with pleasure. Looking up, we realized we had an onlooker, an older guy was peeking over the toilet cubicle walls and obviously wanking on the other side, loving it, hehe nice

I've always been a bit of an exhibitionist, as you'd probably noticed by now, and always aim to please my on-lookers, so as the show-man I am, I pulled out my cummy cock from the guy's bumhole, pushed the boy down on the bare toilet seat, and shoved my cock in his face; and he started licking up the last drops of cum still oozing out of my cock. Cleaning it well with his mouth, and licking my balls while wanking himself off and shooting his load on the floor. We could hear the older man above us getting close and I looked up to see his face in an orgasmic spasm when he shot his load against the toilet partition next to us.

I have to admit there were more boys/men this week, but I'll tell you about them another time, till next time guys, wank a lot and fuck even more... haha

All the best till next week, keep it cumming!

Hugs
Anton

Readers online comments:

I - Saw you on the Overground on Friday, looking hot but weary, no doubt after a long days fucking!

II - I would love to be in a short movie/artwork like this one

III - Why not come to East Yorkshire? David Hockney Country... As beautiful as your imagery and imagination. X

IV - Awesome, amazingly , enchantingly artistic. I could watch this imaginatively, engaging visual chemistry until it stimulates every sense in mind body and spirit. Total respect.

V - Thanks guys, much appreciated, and much love. Anyone want to be filmed for some of my art projects please contact me through my blog and I'll get back to you. I'm also on twitter nowadays: @AntonDicksonX   Hugs a

VI - I rather enjoy reading about your encounters! I'm rock hard!

WEEK   III

OOPS I SAID TOO MUCH

Hi All - This week has been a very interesting one. For the first time in a while, I found myself on the other side of the lens, taking on the role of still photographer and 2nd cameraman for a porn shoot, Directed by Mike Esser (RIP). Well five shoots, actually, over three days only.

I'm not going to bore you with the details but I will say this; I learned a lot, as I was in well over my head in terms of technical lack of knowledge etc regarding the filming aspects (I'm - at least at this point - more of a stills photographer). In particular I learned what NOT to say to guys on set during shoots...

The last shooting day - the Directors monumentally bad "comment slip" was to a model, that'd been in all five scenes over the last three days. It came after approximately 1 hour of intense wanking for the final cumshot. I was bored and ready to go, and clearly so was the Director, so he gets up from behind his camera and simply asked "What time is your last train?" "8PM", the model replied. To which the Director said "Oh you just missed it." Poor guy got an instant soft dick. Needless to say, no cumshot for at least two-three hours...

Anyhow, after the shoot I was bursting with hormones and being in the naughty club land district Vauxhall, I had no difficulty finding eager, horny boys. On my way to the train home, I popped around the corner to the little park behind the station and had two boys follow me. One was very tall and skinny, the other a bit shorter and stockier.

The park didn't have much to offer in terms of bushes, but there was a small little hill that gave a bit of privacy. It was fairly dark anyhow, so I saw no problem taking the two of them back for a little fun there. As soon as we were in position, they both got down on their knees and eagerly started sucking me off. Shortly after they began, the tall boy pulled out a massive cock from his trousers and I knew I just had to have a go at it. I pulled him up and went down on my knees in the wet grass, I began sliding his meat deep down my throat.

He was yummy, and perfect, so I asked if he would let me film him for my new "KUK" project. He was very eager, so I gave him my number. Just as I handed him my card, I lost control of my cock and shot a huge load in the stocky boy's mouth. What a great end to the day. I zipped up, bid the boys farewell and headed back to wait for my train.

When I arrived home, I was still a bit horny but as it was a holiday, my Dad was waiting for me at my flat, visiting from Sweden. You know how it is - when you can't invite someone over, you get even hornier. Of course, later that night I got a text from my local "bus-boy" who wanted to stop by.

Being resourceful, I had him meet me in the basement (which is an empty garage where I happen to do a lot of model test shoots that you can see on my photography site). We went inside the electrical cupboard and before the door could even close, he pulled my throbbing cock out and began sucking me off. It was hot but I wanted more, so I bent him over, spat on my cock and fucked his tight hole until I spunked a big load in his horny ginger cum-dumpster. Letting him out the back door, I popped into the shop to get a bottle of milk (my excuse to my Dad for leaving the flat). Hehe classic.

Tonight I will be heading to the local sauna for some horny action. I love using those gloryholes they have there - they give me such pleasures. My adventures there should lead to some fun stories to share with you next weekend.

Here is a very naughty self filmed scene I did last month with a boy who takes cock so very well. Hope you like it. (See my x-tube link at back of book).

Hugs
Anton

Readers online comments:

I - I can only imagine how raunchy and dirty the sex clubs are over in Europe! I bet the craziest things go on in the back alleys and basements. I want to visit.

II - I bet it must be so much fun to work in the porn industry! I watch it everyday. I can only imagine what it would be like to actually get paid to film it! SO JEALOUS!!

III - Maybe you should make a movie and see how it goes...

IV - That movie looks like it's gonna be hot as fuck

WEEK IV

THE SAUNA EXPERIENCE

This week has been an interesting one. I didn't feel very sexual at all at the start of the week. I had some very quiet nights in, catching up on my favorite fantasy/sci-fi tv-series. It was wonderful. Then all of a sudden my horniness just kicked into high gear again. It's interesting how that happens. I had a very great encounter with a sweet boy who came over - we shared some really nice moments together. He was adorably cute, and we fell asleep naked (spooning) while watching Star Trek.

A few days later a friend mentioned that on Mondays at his gym, (which is also a local gay sauna it turns out, how convenient...) there is free or at least cheaper admission for guys under 25. I thought to myself, I could get in for free - ha, kidding, I'm way past that age thank goodness.

But I thought, why not give it a try, I do like a younger bum to play with now and again, so I made my way over there. Just after entering I realized how busy it really was. I had only been to this sauna once before, and that time it was deserted. Almost instantly I found myself getting felt up by a tall teenage boy with a sweet bum. I took him into one of the cubicles where I pushed him down on his knees to suck my fat throbbing uncut cock. He seemed to enjoy it thoroughly. I pulled him up and bent him over the high bench and spread his legs wide apart so I could have a better look at his bumhole. After rimming him good I put my fat cock in and started fucking him hard. He yelped in pain but pushed hard against me, forcing my cock deeper inside him. By this time we had a bit of an audience, and they were all watching intently while jerking off. It was a fun little show I have to admit. I turned him over and continued fucking him till he came all over himself, then he got up and left straight away.

Now I was really horny, and felt like being a dirty cum whore myself. The boy had left the door a bit open, and I saw a short hairy older guy with a nice sized cock standing outside wanking. His cock wasn't too huge, which I was glad to see when I waved him over. Being more of a top in my later sexual 'career', I can't really take a big cock in my tight hole any longer. I sat up on the bench where the boy had been sitting, laying back in his newly milked puddle of cum and sweat. I pulled the older hairy man in towards me and it reminded me of when I was a young bottom boy many, many years ago.

The older man was into it, and he was pressing himself up against me. I could feel his cock pulsating on my hole... My hole was so tight, and I could feel the familiar, but so forgotten stinging and exciting pain of his cockhead slightly entering me. I pushed him away with my strong dancers legs, but kept wanking myself off, pulling him back with my other arm every once in a while. As a former ballet dancer I have very strong legs, so I finally pulled him towards me one last time, and in it went, all the way. The pain and pleasure was soooo intense I came after only 2 strokes of his cock deep inside me.

I kissed him briefly, and pulled away, smiling shyly. Then I went upstairs for a shower and jacuzzi. In the water I watched two young lovers tightly entwined in an intense embrace. They were kissing passionately, and it was very beautiful to watch. I was tired though, so I went for another shower, and in there was a tall black/mixed man I had met many years ago. He has one of the biggest cocks I have ever come across in my life, and I've seen a lot of cocks. I mean a lot... I said hi, but instead of shaking his outstretched hand, I reached out and shook his huge dick. He said "Oh, hi, hehe" and he instantly got hard. I kept shaking it a bit and I said "That's how we say "hi" in Swedish. Didn't you know?"

Another boy standing close to us in the shower saw us, and reached out to shake my now semi hard cock as he said "Oh hi there, I'm Tom. Nice to meet you." I looked at him and smiled. He was a very cute British guy. All three of us started to kiss and suck each other off as the water rained down on us from the shower. But I changed my mind, so I made my excuses and went for a piss instead haha.

One of the other guys I also played with in the sauna, was a nice normal looking Turkish guy with an average sized cock. He was sitting wanking all by himself in the video room. He looked a bit lonely and sad, so I went over to sit next to him, then started wanking. I reached out to play with his cock and he looked so happy to get someone's attention. It turned me on so much that I couldn't help bending over and sucking him off till he came a massive load in my mouth, yum yum.

Anyhow, after three more shags I finally left exhausted but fully satisfied. Oh and its a special week this week, as my best friend and flatmate (international porn star Dean Monroe) is Launching his self biographical book "Dean Monroe's World" on Wednesday, with images and anecdotes from his varied porn life and beyond (the book also includes a lot of the photos I've taken of him over the years). I thought I would also share this little video I made (with the help of my awesome friend and porn master Liam Cole). I hope you like it. (See links on last pages.) All the best till next week, keep it cumming!

Hugs
Anton

Readers online comments:

I - It is truly a different sex culture over in Europe than it is in the US. More open and free. The men just seem to lose all their inhibitions.

II - Will go to London within a few weeks... which sauna was it?

III - hehe yeah I guess its a bit different over here hehe, the sauna is called 'Sweatbox', close to Oxford Circus, hugs a

WEEK V

POLAR BEAR FIGHT

A lot of thoughts this week. The biggest thing is that I really miss my best friend, soulmate, flatmate, etc. - Dean Monroe. He's away for three months in LA, and there's always an empty gap when he's away, but no sad faces here. I did a really fun shoot at the start of the week with a new company I haven't worked with before, they sell their stuff to Prowlers. I got to fuck two hot twink boys, which is always fun. We were double fucking one of the guys. I also fucked one while he fucked the other and then I lined them up, one on top of the other, giving them turns on my fat cock, pulling it out of one bum and pushing it into the other one directly after. Very horny fun, indeed!

The only thing, though, was that the owners of the flat we filmed in, had two long haired furry white cats, and in the living room where we were shooting there was also a really furry white carpet. We were soooooo covered in long cat hair and carpet hair by the end of the shoot, one could have thought a polar bear fight had just taken place. Not recommended, hehe. I even coughed up a furball (at the same time as the cat did when I entered the kitchen naked), classy haha...

On the way back from the late evening shoot something happened. I was walking fast to get the last train back into central town, to go home, and it was raining heavily (usual London weather), when a black girl ran out in front of me, screaming hysterically, obviously really upset. She dragged me towards a man lying down in a puddle of water, sort of paralysed, with a bottle of what seemed to be coca cola mixed with something in his hand. The black girl was trying to pull him up, telling me she just walked past him when he collapsed. I bent over to have a closer look at the man.

When I got closer, an extremely handsome young man's face (turned out he was 21) looked up at me, obviously so drunk he didn't have a clue where he was or what he was doing. The boy was completely drenched and dirty, so I tried to help him up in a sitting position. When I turned around to look for the black girl to see if she could help me get him up, she was nowhere to be seen...

The boy was telling me stuff, babbling - his mum had recently died, that's why he was drinking and he had sleeping pills, etc. I got very sad. I started to call an ambulance to see if I could get him some help, but he wouldn't have any of it. After that he seemed to calm down a bit. I sat with him for half an hour, talking with him. By this time I had managed to get him to sit on the steps of a church nearby, out of the rain. He had one of those faces that sticks with you for a long time. I explained to him that I had to leave him there, as my train was going to leave in 10 min. I felt so horrible for leaving him there all by himself. His face has been on my mind all week, I really hope he is OK. I wish I could do more for others here in life, and that I had thousands of arms to support others, hugs for everyone.

A couple of days after that, I shot an amazing hot scene for Liam Cole with awesome Italian model Jake Ascott, which I'm sure all you horny buggers out there will love. He has a SWEET bum and a nice big fat cock which I loved sucking. Fuck, he is one hotty boy! I'm sure we will see more of him on the TIM sites and elsewhere. I also got a message on a chat line from a young boy asking me: "Do you know how 2 pleasure?" Hm, lets see - what shall I answer? You can see some photos of me in my blog archive, one from the local leather shop where I was photographing customers trying on outfits for a promotion thingy, which was good fun. I do love wearing my Swedish clogs, haha. Not sure they go so well with small leather shorts though, but who gives a fuck right?

There are also photos of me and my best mate Dean Monroe, where I look completely fucked lol. Although I don't drink or do drugs, I do make a good impression of it, haha.

Here is a little music video "Greedy Eyes" I directed and produced, a self-funded project which was shown at the

Berlin Porn Film Festival in autumn last year. It was great to make - I had such an awesome day, with an amazing team, cast and crew. Thanks to everyone involved. (For photos and videos see links at end.)

Till next time!
Hugs Anton

Readers online comments:

I - Thanks Anton. Love all of the updates.

II - Anything Treasure Island puts out there is always a hit in my books.

III - Downloaded the uncensored version with the gorgeous fuckscene which amazingly was on youtube for a few days before it got deleted. Thanx for making such an amazing clip

IV - hehe thanks mr, glad u liked it, hugs anton

WEEK VI

A CUMWHORE IS BORN

Today I thought we should have a little sexual history lesson, going all the way back to Anton Dickson's first "proper" gay sexual encounter. I found myself in Paris, France at the tender age of 17 with my then - girlfriend of a few months (we were very innocent and had only really been kissing, being politely Swedish and restrained). We were both dancers - she was very flexible and so was I, and I had often fantasized of what we could get up to if and when we actually got to it, so to speak.

We were taking summer classes in Les Marais (famous for its gay bars, which I had no knowledge of at the time, of course), studying hard at Centre de Danse du Marais, an old and rundown studio surrounding a picturesque old courtyard. The whole atmosphere was truly magic, with a little cafe in the yard and everyone speaking sexy French everywhere.

The sun was shining through the ballet studios dirty windows and highlighted a very handsome, Cuban guy who was an incredible dancer, so flexible yet so strong, with the biggest bulge in his jockstrap I had ever seen. Standing on the opposite side of the barre, I couldn't help but look at him as often as I could, bending backwards, flicking my head towards him in the small pirouettes, etc. He obviously noticed this and smiled coyly towards me, knowing something I didn't know it seemed. I was very innocent in those days: I didn't think of him in a sexual way, just thought he was a great dancer and guy, just truly fascinating.

The lesson ended and my girlfriend, who'd just made friends with some Parisian girls, came to tell me they were going shopping for some new point shoes. I didn't mind at all, as I watched the handsome Cuban dancer, gathering his stuff and leaving the studio. I followed suite and entered the dressing room after him, where he started undressing. I went into the shower to see if I could see a bit of his obviously massive cock. He must have felt my stare, as he slowly turned around, face first, hips last, revealing a humongous cock totally out of proportion with his lean, slim, well-trained physique and 8-pack. "Wow", I said (I couldn't help it). He laughed at me, soaped it up and turned away from me, the water caressing his sweet bum. When I was getting dressed and packing up my bag, he came over to me. "Wanna come over to my place and watch a ballet video?"He asked. I said sure (I was so naive that I actually thought we were only going to watch a DVD - little did I know). "What do you have, anything with Baryshnikov? He's my favourite". I said. He just laughed and smiled. We left the studio; the sun was sparkling in his eyes.

Well in his flat he turned on the telly and put on a Baryshnikov video. I was hypnotised - his jumps, his pirouettes - such an amazing, strong male dancer. I didn't even notice the Cuban boy sitting down next to me, and all of the sudden he pushed me down on the bed and was on top of me. I was so shocked and surprised I didn't know what to say. "What are you d..?" He shushed me and lowered his lips to mine. His big lower lip was salty, and felt amazing. He kissed me so passionately I lost track of everything around me. I succumbed completely to his touch - he was all over me, we were naked as if by magic, and his hands and kisses were everywhere. I felt a pleasure I had never felt before. It was such an amazing moment, I will always treasure it.

And the climax was not a fucking (oh no, I was far too innocent back than for that, hehe). No, it was me on my knees in front of his fantastic, big cock (he was 21 - and experienced) and him shooting a HUGE load all over my face and chest and in my mouth. I eagerly licked it up, as much as I could fit in my mouth, the sweat taste of his cum, and as soon as I tasted it I knew that this I wanted more of, as much as I could get in fact. In other words, a true cum-whore was born. The rest is history. When we were in his shower after washing each other off, he asked if I liked that. I was again lost for words of how to describe the strong emotional and physical feeling I had just experienced, and I told him he was my first. "What?

You should have told me, I would have made it special", he said. "Oh, it was special - trust me", I assured him. He smiled, relieved. We left the flat and went down to have a Nutella and banana crepes, my favourite when I'm in Paris from that moment on (still is; it always remind me of that sweat first load in my innocent mouth). The reason I wanted to tell you this little story is that, funnily enough, a couple of months ago I got a message online on one of the chat lines: "Hi there sexy, I don't know if you remember me, but I was your first!" Wow, total flashback, loved it, he now lives in New York and works as an escort.

On another note, Spring is in the air today. London was so warm and uncharacteristically sunny, I loved it - all the hotties were out en masse in their T-shirts on my lunchbreak, showing off as they should, hehe, and here I'm sitting relaxing and eating a pork belly and apple sauce sandwich. Loving it. Some pics of me in my new and awesome TIM vest on my blog. (Mitch told me that Americans call them tank tops) Hope you like it! P.S. I just found out that I will get to fuck TIM's awesome exclusive model Jackson when I go to LA in June. I'm so looking forward to playing with his sweet horny boyhole!

Hugs Anton

Readers online comments:

I - I can't wait to be able to watch Anton fuck Jackson!! I can only imagine how hot it's going to be.

II - I love how he compared Nutella to his first load of cum! Two of my favorite things as well!! haha

III - hehe Nutella cum, oh I can see a new marketing strategy for Nutella, nice... hehe

IV - very hot .....

WEEK VII

WANK HOLIDAY

This week we had a bank holiday weekend here in London. My understanding of bank holidays is that you are supposed to rest and be lazy and be a couch potato (which I'd love to do, but I'm far too impatient for that). I went to an art/architecture event for one of my closest friends from my student days. It was a very busy event. As usual at such gatherings, there's a lot of pompous, "Ah, oh, that's interesting", and, "Oh, so what you trying to say with this dot and few lines is that the infinity of the universe lies at the bottom of the sea, blah blah," which usually goes way over my head.

But, strangely enough, it does make me extremely horny, and I just feel like ripping out my fat cock and show it to everyone, oops. (Don't get too excited now, though. At this occasion I didn't, mainly as I didn't want to embarrass my friend, though she probably wouldn't have minded). On the way home from the event, after having dinner with my good friend and neighbour, I decided to invite a guy I've been chatting to on Grindr for quite some time, who's also an architect. I'd never met up with him before. He came over, and we were watching telly and talked; he didn't want to play sexually, as he's neg and a bit worried, which is understandable.

I then got a message from another boy whom I'd chatted with before but never met. I invited him over and the architect asked if I wanted him to leave. "No, why?" I said. "You can stay and watch." He was keen on this idea.

The hot horny young boy arrived - a bit high, I guess, as almost before he was in the door, all his clothes were off and he was sucking my growing cock. My friend curiously watched the boy's amazing blowjob technique, swallowing the whole of my fat 8-inch cock. "Should we not close the curtains?" The architect said, looking at my full height floor to ceiling glazed corner windows on the 5th floor. "Nah, it's alright, no one can see us, they'll just see the reflections," I said, thinking to myself that a lot of lights were on in the flat.

I started fucking the boy's horny bum, rimming his ass and kissing him passionately. I looked up, and realized the architect had stripped right down as well and was wanking hard now. "Wanna join in?" I asked politely. He declined but continued wanking, transfixed with watching my fat cock in the boy's horny hole.

Shortly after he came - a big nice load, which he teased the bottom boy with but wouldn't let him taste. "Next time, maybe..." he said, and pulled on his clothes and left. I continued fucking the boy for another two hours, shooting three big loads up his horny hole and in his mouth; he cleaned my cock with his eager mouth between each time. Exhausted, we fell asleep in each others arms. "Wake me up at 6, I have to go to work", was the last he said. I looked at the clock, realizing it was almost 4am... oh well.

The boy left in the morning and I fell asleep again, enjoying the sound of the rain hitting hard against my window. I woke up again at 8am, when I got a message from a hot and very horny regular shag buddy of mine, a sexy Polish boy, who was in the area. He'd been up fucking for 15 hours, but just wanted one more load before going home to sleep it all off. Fifteen minutes later, he was laid on my sofa with his bare bum out, shoes and the rest of his clothes still on, moaning with my big fat cock up his horny hole.

I could feel the stickiness of the other lads' horny loads up his hole, smelling the strong sent of cum mixed with sweat, so fucking horny. I came quickly and the boy left. After eating some grapes and Brazil nuts (which are really good for your CD4 counts btw, as they contain natural Selenium), I went back to bed.

I woke up just before 12 and started setting up my photography studio, as I was renting it out to a young sexy photographer friend of mine. He was going to photograph a sexy escort. They arrived together with another photographer, and the shoot seemed to go well. I do love having naked guys in my flat, especially if they are as hung as this horny looking Italian escort was...

After the shoot I had a guy over, and again fucked him on the sofa. He wasn't that good and after he left, I was still feeling horny, so I logged on to Grindr. I started to chat to a guy, who turned out to be my neighbour across the street. "Are you in the building above Tesco?" he asked. "Yeah I am, on the fifth floor," I said. "And you are a pornstar?" he asked. "Well I've been in a few films yeah" I said. "You might have seen me fucking on the couch the other day..." throwing it out there to see what he said. "Wow, was that you, my flatmate's girlfriend saw you guys and told us about it. She thought you had a good rhythm, it was fucking horny to watch - you should invite me over sometimes..." Fuck, that was horny. I always love being a bit of an exhibitionist - fun times, indeed, hehe.

The rest of the weekend sums up as this: Dinner in town with my old two flatmates and my old ballet partner from Sweden and her best friend, awesome fun, lots of Golden Duck. Then I licked a horny dancer's sexy butthole till he squashed my head tight with his strong thighs and came a horny big load all over my beard (protein diet for everyone... haha). After that I played with a horny Canadian dancer friend of mine, who has a very nice cock and will hopefully film with Liam Cole soon.

Oh, I almost forgot: I also launched my first Photography book this week. It features photographs of young male models/boys on their first steps into the tough male modeling world. You can find the hard copy at blurb.com and also the iPad/iPhone version — at a much discounted rate. You can see more photos on my blogs in the archive... (blasts from the past). Hope you like them.

Btw, Liam just showed me a little clip from his new DVD, SLAMMED. Fucking hell, it looks sooooooooo hot and horny, can't wait to see it. More about it next week... promise.

Hugs
Anton

Readers online comments:

I - This story might be the hottest thing I've ever read. I couldn't even imagine having that much sex. Anton is truly a god amongst men!!

II - Hehe thanks Trey, Well I was always very sexual, If you think this is a lot lol hm u should have seen me when I was 20 lol, (I'm 36 now), I used to cum on average 5-8 times a day, and I would say the majority of time was not wanks... That's a story for another week though as there are some fun memories to tell indeed hehe. Hugs anton

III - I am an architect too, can I watch? You have a nice veiny cock :-)

IV - Hi Anton, I just wanted to say I have seen tons of porn in my time. Mainly on treasure island. The all time far out best ever was you fucking Adam King. I have no idea how many times I have watched the entire thing at half speed with a bottle of poppers and had the best time. Thank you. Ps also in London. Also 36 also horny and beautiful, would love to meet. Where do you hang out?

V - Hey there, well thank you mr, yeah that was a hot scene indeed, and I love horny beautiful 36 years olds, I live in Haggerston, but don't 'hang out' a lot, I'm too busy to go clubbing / bars nowadays, but catch me on facebook, and lets take it from there sexy hehe, (I'm Anton Dickson on facebook).

WEEK VIII

ROUGH; INTENSE; SLAMMED

Hey, good men and boys. This week my great friend and awe-some director at TIM London, Liam Cole, showed me a little teaser clip from his new DVD, SLAMMED which is coming out in the fall. It showed a great, very passionate and intense sequence between sexy Keiran (on the left) and horny, gorgeous Jon Phelps (on the right).

From my computer screen I instantly felt the rough-ness and the intensity between them, and the hungry kissing aroused me immediately. True horny, raw kissing is some-thing you don't often see in gay porn, I find, and it only re-ally happens when the chemistry is right. I really can't wait to watch the full video, will be sooo horny hehe. I think Liam is a true master in setting up and capturing these horny scenes, and it's always fun to work with him. I had to have a few wanks watching that little clip, and you can also see it below - hotttt!!! Can't wait to see the whole DVD.

Other than that, awesome TIM exclusive Christian was in town and I got to shoot a scene with him and big-cocked Rob Tyler. Fucking Christian's horny bumhole on my couch, in full view of my neighbours, hehe, naughty! Apart from that, this week has been pretty quiet. I rented out my photo studio to a few nude shoots over the weekend; as usual, I do enjoy the naked boys in my flat, as I'm sure you can imagine.

Tonight I'm shooting a threesome for a small new studio with some sexy young twink boys (Mike Preston and Fernando). I do enjoy a naughty boy to play with, but be aware it's the polar-bear house, so I'll be coughing up furballs again - wish me luck... To the left is a picture of the sexy Mike Preston. And the day after tomorrow I'm doing more shoots for Liam with a German new model, I believe; it will be fun, fun, fun. Oh, I found these pics of me and hot model Felix Barca from a shoot we did in Berlin a year ago for CAZZO (check the blog archive). Such a shame he doesn't take it BB.

Many hugs and horny KISSES
Suck those lips hard
Anton Dickson

Readers online comments:

I - Wow, fucking hot scene! That guy is so slammed! Wish it was me in his place!

II - Slammed in more ways than one by the looks of this...

III - I love hearing about Anton's scenes! Please keep them coming.

IV - Jon Phelps is fucking gorgeous!

V - I think some people will love it and others will find it disturbing. But that could be said of a lot of TIM's stuff over the years.

VI - I want to be in a video like this as the pig btm.

VII - horny for slammed DVD hehe, soon folks, soon...

VIII - I am so grateful to Jon and Keiran for that night. For me, the intensity of this SLAMMED clip is what making porn is all about.

IX - Cool! I bet its going to be very very good!

X - Been working on it today, and it's coming on nicely

XI - Cant wait for Slammed!

CHRONICLES OF A LONDON CUMPIG

WEEK IX

TOILETS AND ORGIES

This week I dedicate to TOILETS and ORGIES, the first of which has always been a passion of mine, even before I actually had any gay sex. I told you my first proper sexual encounter in a previous blog entry but even before that, when I was 16 and moved to Stockholm from a small suburban north Swedish town, there were many hidden treasures to discover.

One of these treasures, which I would often go and watch, although not partake in, were the pissoirs [public urinals] at the local central station in Stockholm. The toilets were "hidden" away from the usual commuters, around the corner of the luggage area on the basement floor, out of sight and out of thought of most busy big city people rushing around.

I used to go in there, stand in the stinking (it truly stank so strongly of piss it was hard to bear, but a deep desire in me persuaded me to stay) pissoir and cubicles, with the typical "separation" panels in between, all in stainless steel. The partitions were covered in writings like "suck my cock", "dirty boy needs load", "pay for suck/fuck fun", followed by a whole array of telephone numbers and scribbles. The crude drawings of cocks and bums getting penetrated by ever larger cocks on the walls and partitions, fascinated me.

There were very seldom any guys in there but it didn't matter; the whole atmosphere was just sex and I used to go there and wank (from age 16 and till I left Stockholm when I was 18-19). One of my favourite places to cum was on one of the scribble paintings that someone had so cleverly done in an area of the wall that was damaged and had a gaping hole in it. Drawn around it was a face with an eager mouth waiting for the load, where I must have emptied at least a couple of loads a week.

I remember the first time I actually met anyone in there: I was just about to shoot my load when the metal door opened. The guilty look on my face made the old man who was entering smile a quirky smile. "Don't let me stop you," he said in Swedish to me, and I relaxed and continued wanking. The man took out his cock and I was surprised to see how big it was. Fascinated by looking at it, I shot my load, missing the mouth in the wall. Just as I was walking past the man, he reached out to touch me but I shied away, rushed towards the door and was gone. A couple of days later I was back again, of course, wanking and wishing that someone might walk in on me again...

Anyhow, back to the present. I did a shoot for Liam Cole on Friday, a little threesome in a dark sex club environment. (They have spanking nights, piss nights, etc. Those aren't scenes I usually get into so much myself, but I'm always up for trying new things; however, this was not such a scene). In the middle of the scene, the bottom lad - a muscled, hairy French lad - got down on his knees on the dirty floor, poking his hot arse up towards me and the other top, a short but big-dicked Spanish guy, yummy.

Liam is going to kill me for telling you this, but I thought it was sooo funny (and crazy all at once) that I can't help from sharing this: I didn't notice anything at the time and I don't think the other lads noticed anything either, but Liam told me after the shoot that less than half a meter from the kneeling guys face was a dead cockroach laying on his back. Liam - discretely - so as not to interrupt the action - kicked it to the opposite side of the room, and everything continued like nothing had happened, hehe. Oh, the things we experience in porn... always fun, lol. (The shoot was with Enzo and Priam, btw).

After that we went back to the TIM London office, where I got to meet our awesome new assistant Ashton Bradley, who has just started helping us out with the admin and booking of models etc. A very nice guy, indeed. We need to get him a TIM bag and jumper now; suited and booted, as they say, hehe. Welcome onboard! On the same evening as the cockroach shoot, Liam was filming a group orgy in my flat. I was too exhausted to join in, but it's always fun having naked boys running around my flat and the smell of sex - ooh la la. The horny German/Greek bottom lad was so loud I think even Ashton, on the other side of town, heard him scream in pain and pleasure after receiving some of the big fat cocks Liam had lined up for him. Meanwhile I was trying to concentrate and upload my reduced size photography book, Atelier A-Z MINI.

You can see it on my weblinks at end of this book. I also updated my website , including the video section and the full size version of my book. It's looking mighty fine, I have to admit, hehe - blush.

The rest of the weekend I spent catching up on "Revenge" and "Once Upon a Time". I'm such a child at heart, hehe. Oh, and I had a little wank today (well, actually, three in a row - but I only filmed the first one) on my couch, and almost instantly I got a message from my lovely, hot, pervy neighbour across the road saying, "Wanking again?" Hehe, love it - he kept talking me through the wank saying what turned him on and stuff. So horny, loved it, I really DO have to invite him over sometime, at least to watch me fuck some horny boy. Anyone up for having a horny fuck and a sexy onlooker? (Who knows, he might even wank while watching us hehe, nice.)

Oh, I also got fucked the other day, almost forgot about that. It was rather unexpected but pleasant all the same. The busboy turned up on my doorstep unannounced on Sunday morning, and demanded I sucked him off. And who am I to deny such a sweet, hot ginger boy a horny time? Then I let him fuck me too, and ouch, was I in pain on Monday morning, lol. Till next

Hugs Anton

Readers online comments:

I - Cum on boys, u should all cum and we'll show you around hehe.

II - I'm meeting a cutie from Birmingham! London is definitely somewhere I plan on going. Hope I get a nice welcome!

III - You're such a gent Anton, offering to let your neighbour come over and watch you fuck someone live. Who says community spirit is dead?

IV - The thought of having a hot neighbor watch you shag some horny bottom boy is really enticing! Please blog it if does happen in detail! =) Cheers

V - Hehe, yeah its fucking horny I tell u hehe, I sometimes see him across the windows watching me close up to his windows wanking, and I sit on couch watching porn and wanking too, hehe, awesome...

CHRONICLES OF A LONDON CUMPIG

WEEK   X

TUTORIALS

Oh the mighty tutorials... This week's blog I dedicate to the ancient role of tutors and tutorials, whether it be learning how to walk, how to talk or how to suck cock well, let's skip the crap. It's basically just about the sucking cock tutorial, hehe. I'm not sure if it's me getting older and less patient but I often find myself, rather than suffering at the cock end of a bad blow-job, voicing my suggestions of how the guy should go about it. Blow-jobs are a fine art: not too hard, not too soft, not too repetitive but repetitive enough for stimulation, etc etc.

Then there are so many different types of cocks, all needing stimulation in slightly different ways, and I'm not just talking about the two main differences (cut vs. uncut). This last week I've been holding tutorials in the art of cock-sucking for a local mixed-race guy who works close to my office. He's been coming in and kneeling down in the toilet cubicles at work, in front of my 8 inches of man meat, eagerly anticipating the next tutorial. The first lesson was actually concentrating on the ball-licking technique. Lesson number 2 focused on how to lock eyes with the "cock"-person while still keeping the tongue moving consistently. I have to admit he did very well, hehe.

Today we advanced to deep-throating techniques, which he still needs a bit of practice on. But as they say: practice makes perfect, and eagerness to learn goes a long way. I have to admit that deep-throating on your knees in front of a standing man is not always that easy, depending on the bend of the cock etc. (69ing with the neck over the edge of the bed, with the top standing on his feet leaning over, usually does the trick for the bigger gentlemen, hehe).

As usual this week has been filled with eventful things. The big thing, I guess, was that I started volunteering. It's an independent visitor scheme, where I'm meeting a young man and helping him gain more self confidence, as well as helping with independence living skills such as simple budgeting, shopping, cooking meals, etc. The first meeting went very well and I'm sure we will get on just splendidly; he seems like a really nice person. It's my little way of saying thank you (and helping others in life) to my great foster/adoptive mum for taking care of me when I was just a baby, and ever after - love you, mum! This is something I will be doing approximately once a month for a year's time, at least. So it's a challenge, but a rewarding one.

I also had the great joy of photographing little sexy twink Leo Mack for a Prowler shoot this Tuesday, where he was testing out sex toys of various types, from horny little (and BIG) dildos to massage tools for your cocks, jockstraps, etc. It was very fun and Leo is such a great guy to work with.

I ran into my old flatmate and another Swedish/Norwegian friend of mine in Soho and we lay around Soho Square, just being silly and playing the fools, so much fun. Oh, I almost forgot: I went up to the (in)famous Hampstead Heath (some of you might have heard of Liam Cole's famous award winning DVD that was allegedly filmed on the Heath at night - oh horny thoughts). Enjoying the scorching sunshine and hot bodies laying around on the grass, I felt obliged to go into the nude enclosed section of the men's pond. After a bit of eye-flirting, a cute Asian boy came and sat on the ground literally 2 cm in front of my cock (I was sitting on a bench in the shadow).

After a bit of cock-flicking, it didn't take long for me to drive him crazy and he reached out to grab my cock (to the joy of all the surrounding elder naked gentlemen I must add). Soon the boy was giving me head like a pro, clearly having been taught by an attentive master hehe.

When I left the nude section, one of the onlookers reached up and touched my hand: "Thank you for the show."

It made me blush (no, not really, hehe - but it was funny). This evening I'm packing my bag and printing my boarding passes, as I'm off to Los Angeles (and also Las Vegas) tomorrow. I will be away for two weeks, so next time I'll be writing you from US soil. I'll be filming with Jackson Taylor from TIM, which I'm very much looking forward to - it's sure going to be a lot of fun!

Have a great week, folks, and enjoy the sunshine. (It was 27 degrees Celsius in London last week, so I've been going to work in my little shorts - to the great annoyance of my architect boss. But hey, we are not porn guys for nothing right?

Hugs, Anton

Readers online comments:

I - I need to go to London and meet Anton. He seriously has the hottest and craziest stories.

II - If only tutorials like this were offered in more areas.

III - IF they're true, that is...

IV - definitely true mr hehe, hugs from London.

WEEK XI

MY SoCal ADVENTURE

Hey, guys. So as promised, I'm writing to you from the big country in the West: the USA. I arrived safely to an awesome, hot and sunny California, although while walking on the beach in shorts and tank top, sweating in the sun, some teen-age kids walked past wearing trousers and long sleeves. "It's a bit chilly today," one said to the other. Clearly they haven't been to London - or Sweden, for that matter, haha.

Anyhow, I met up with some of the awesome T.I.M. crew - Pony, Trevor and Nick - to create some T.I.M. magic. I got to meet hot, huuuge Italian model Luca Bondi, and to-gether we fucked a horny bottom lad (don't know his porn name, maybe Mitch knows). It was so fucking sexy sucking his fat cock before and after it going into the lad's hungry hole, and then getting to lick out his load after he came, hehe. I'm getting a stiffy just thinking about it – yum yum.

The day after I got to fuck AWESOME cute twinky bottom and T.I.M. exclusive Jackson Taylor, a horny little Italian boy. It was a fucking hot scene, with my fat uncut cock pounding his sweet little boyhole hard. At one point I was laying back on the bed, catching my breath, and I told him to come lick my balls. He eagerly obliged, crawling up between my legs, licking and sucking my cock. Good boy, I tell you. Before I knew it, he was up riding my cock again, and then Pony helped me hold him down so I could fuck a big load up his sweet little boy hole.

I would sooooooo love to do a threesome scene with me and Luca Bondi taking turns on sweet boy Jackson Tay-lor's horny boy-holes... Make it happen, T.I.M.!

It has so far been a wonderful trip, and today me and my husband are heading up to Las Vegas for some hedonistic fun. Then it's West Hollywood Gay Pride weekend, so watch out, all you horny boys - Anton Dickson is in town! After that it's back to good old rainy Britain, but for now I better put on some sun lotion. Anyone wanna rub me up? You can see some photos from the trip on my blog. Can't wait to share more whore stories with you next week, upon my return.

Hugs, Anton Dickson

Readers online comments:

I - This man is so fucking gorgeous. Gotta love the English!

II - I can only imagine all the trouble he's going to get into this weekend in LA for Pride.

III - Can't wait to be able to watch him fuck Jackson Taylor.

IV - Can Not wait to see more of him.

V - Luca Bondi is hot! want him on team TIM!

VI - Hehe I'm Swedish mix Croatian, if u were referring to me hehe, was a lot of fun at Pride. Yeah I hope it's out soon mate, and yeah he is very sexy, will be in London soon, hopefully get to do another scene with him. hugs anton

CHRONICLES OF A LONDON CUMPIG

WEEK XII

PARK CRUISING, LA PRIDE AND

Hey, all. This week I'm back in a cooler London. Actually it's not that bad, to be honest, but we don't have the Las Vegas sunshine or the Newport beaches, that's for sure hehe.

I watched Liam Cole's awesome Woodland Scene (from the hot DVD Wild Breed) again. It's a scene that always turns me on so much. This time it made me remember some of my naughty French adventures when I lived in Lille after I first moved to France. I was 19, new to the whole gay thing and still mainly dating girls at the time. But by a coincidence I discovered a forest/park area adjacent to a military training campus, in the citadel, surrounded by a fortified river bank (an ideal cruising ground, it turned out).

I still vividly remember the first time I had sex with one of those horny lost military boys: him sneaking out at midnight and me wandering around the forest already. I saw him coming towards me in the moonlight and before he was even up close, he had ripped most of his clothes off. He pressed his cock deep into my mouth and it didn't take long before he shot a welcome load in my eager mouth. We lay back, relaxed and watched the twinkling stars. And then he told me, in broken English with a nice thick French accent, "I want your cock in me." I almost creamed straight away, fucking his smooth horny hole - yummy! As you can surely guess, I returned many a time, looking for that boy, but never saw him again, maybe he was transferred... Then again, there were many other eager boys to please, so I didn't complain too much, hehe.

Los Angeles was lovely, by the way. My hotel was very nice, but a bit small, it turned out it was Gay Pride, so it was filled with gay guys, all happily humping each other away till late hours. America is such a funny place, it's all so - hm, not sure how to describe it - not real? Surreal? Like everything is BIG. The cars are massive for a starter, the roads are even bigger, and the food portions are HUGE... God knows how anyone can finish them in one go, hehe. We went to the cinema, and the area outside was like Disneyland, with jumping water features, plastic looking facades, imitating all sorts of European classical styles, and periods etc.

I mean, it was truly awesome, don't get me wrong. So kitsch, but I loved it. It made me laugh a lot, and the sunshine really brought out a naughty side in me, I have to admit. In Las Vegas, Dino booked us a stretch limo from the airport to the hotel, which was AWESOME! I'd never been in one before; it was sooo cool. We stayed at the fantastic Cosmopolitan Hotel, with its amazing views from the 43rd floor overlooking the jumping water fountains and pools nearby. I fucked some horny boys, and a horny man sucked me off in his room on the 65th floor while his wife was having treatments in the spa area - very hot and naughty, hehe.

We also ventured to a local gay bar and found ourselves invited to the VIP area, which is always fun, and watched a stripper strutting his stuff for our entertainment. (It was good to be on the receiving end, for once. Maybe I should get myself a rentboy soon and tell him what to do - sounds like fun no?) After stripping down to the smallest shorts I could possibly find for LA Gay Pride and walking around on the street in my TIM tank top (that brought many smiles to the naughtier dirty guys), I ended up playing 69 with a very horny looking muscle DJ before heading back to London. And guess what I did as soon as I got back? Well, of course I went to check out my local cruising toilets, got a few blowjobs, and there we were: back in business again, haha.

I love this town, so easy to get good head, (easier than in the U.S. it seems, though that was probably because I don't know where to go yet there. Someone teach me please, hehe.) You can find some photos on in the blog archives.

Hugs anton

Readers online comments:

I - The big size of things in the USA some say is a direct response to the first Great Depression.

II - Was a very fun trip indeed

WEEK XIII

ROCK HARD CINEMA FUN

So to another week of naughtiness. This week started with a little gay birthday party held by a friend of a friend, where the creme de la creme of London gay men gathered to celebrate his birthday in true style and decadence, munching on Pavlova and cheesecake while drinking champagne. I was, as usual, on a strict non-alcoholic sprite regime. It was, indeed, a fun evening; however, I shall not linger on this, as it's truly too predicable for "gay" fun, as they say. As usual, I had a few blowjobs in the local cruising toilets, at the tube station I walk past to work. A few talented mouths and a few that needed a bit of gentle instruction for improvements; nothing out of the ordinary, just a man's daily need taken care of, hehe.

The surprise was one evening when me and my best friend went to the cinema. He was running a bit late and, after getting the ticket, I hung around the toilets (I know classy right, lol, but it beats Grindr at times, I promise!). I hadn't been there long before a horny ginger boy in his late teens entered. One glance was all it took and he knew we were in business. He pulled out a nice-sized, cut cock, and I was down on my knees, sucking it, before he managed to pull out his big hanging balls. He was moaning quite loudly so I had to tell him to be quiet as this was a public loo, after all, and usually quite busy after each screening.

He pulled me up after a while and went down on me, which felt so good, I was rock hard. While he was sucking me, I got a text from my mate wondering were I was. I texted back that I was having a dump, but I was just about to dump my load in the boys mouth... And as soon as he could taste my sweet juice, he shot his load over the urinal - hot, creamy, white spunk. I bent over to taste some of his load, sweet boy juice still oozing out of his cock. After that we both zipped up and he gave me a coy smile, said he had to get back to his girlfriend, and went back into the cinema; I went out to see my friend, who was patiently waiting downstairs.

The day after I was back at the cinema, as I had found an un-used ticket to the VIP seats and thought, why not to use it? It turned out the film was utter rubbish and I walked out after 25 min of pure agony (I rarely walk out on films, but this one I couldn't handle, hehe). I thought, why not pop into the toilets again to see if I could find any fun? Lucky me, a hot hairy guy in his mid 30s was standing there. He glanced in my direction when I entered and I didn't need more of an invitation: I went down on my knees in front of him and sucked him, good and deep, till he shot a big load in my eager mouth. It tasted sweet, I'm sure he'd had a cappuccino just before - I could taste coffee in the cum hehe. Anyhow, I asked him when he last got a blowjob and he said 8 weeks. Apparently that one was by a girl who couldn't deep throat, nor swallow cum, nor lick balls, wtf???

Happily I left the cinema. I love the entertainment they serve there... The area it's situated in is called Angel - how suitable, hehe. No wonder straight guys are completely sexually frustrated and needs to get drunk every other day to stay happy, hehe I would be an alcoholic too if I didn't get my daily blow-jobs (kidding)! But seriously, girls really need to learn about male sexuality and how it functions, much more than men need to learn about female sexuality, hehe.

Today I got several messages from a horny straight guy I used to see a couple of years ago. He's around 28, I think, I was the first guy that sucked his cock (for all I know I might still be the only guy that has sucked his cock); can't remember if I told you all about him before.

Tomorrow I'm off to the clinic, always fun, and see who I can chat up there this time (or would that be 'inap-propriate' hehe?). And guys, remember to eat your two (max. 3, no more) Brazil nuts a day, to keep the doctor away and a high CD4 count up (it contains natural selenium which is very good for your immune system). Just a little tip for today. See u all soon. Also, I'll be starting to prepare for my Prague visit soon - watch out, all you Czech boys, here I come!

Hugs - Anton

Readers online comments:

I - I want to move to London! I've loved every single film. out of the UK with these guys!

II - It's Awesome, well the weather sucks lol/ Follow me on twitter, hugs anton

III - Each time I watch a Treasure Island, TIM, or Morris, on line I become a sex maniac. Instant erection time.

IV - I love every movie from TIM/ I became a sex BB addict because of TIM/ Awesome! I want to be part of you, (TIM), such as an porno-actor, YEAH! Love it! Hugs & Kisses!

V - Darn wish we had a cinema like this in the U.S.

WEEK   XIV

the CZECH COUNTRYSIDE ADVEN-

Hello Sexy TIM - Fans and Horny Men - This week I'm writing you from the Czech countryside just outside of Prague. Where I'm filming some scenes for an independent new bareback porn company, selling their scenes to Prowlers etc. We left from an unusually hot London in two cars (one 7 seater and one 5 seater), pulling a trailer with bags and camera equipment. We were almost full capacity in the car, making it a very crowded car, filled with twinky boys... The journey went very well though, crossing the English channel by ferry (eating tasteless, overpriced sausages, ofcourse hehe) and passing through northern France and south of Germany.

The only stops we made was to fill up with petrol and to empty our balls, pissing only hehe. Having the little trailer limited our speed drastically, which meant a very long journey; we reached a steaming hot Prague 24 hours after leaving London. By this time we were all sweaty and a bit grumpy I have to admit.

We stayed at a nice hotel adjacent to a large arena, and after a Mac Donalds 'nutritious' meal we started a few shoots, believe it or not... We were all so tired, I was starting to fuck two guys (they were a couple) but they decided they couldn't shoot together or something, so we didn't manage to finish the scene. Not a problem for me though; there's always a next time, but it was a bit frustrating still, I'm always a believer of finishing of a job / project properly ones I've started it.

I tried to chat up the sexy boy working at the Mac Donalds around the corner of the hotel, a very hot Czech guy, but without success unfortunately, hehe. The following day, after a two hours drive, we reached our destination - a very large country house in the middle of no-where, surrounding a little cute grass courtyard. By this time we had also been joined by a very cute French boy, a hung Czech guy and an American twinky boy and his "Master". This is where all the fun started, hehe. We quickly settled into our new rooms and ran for the pool to cool down, was so nice to relax properly for a bit, than we tried the jacuzzi also hehe.

We've been shooting two to three scenes per day, in different areas of the house: the cool inside pool - that opens up onto the internal closed-of courtyard grass patch, the billiard table room (that was just under the tiled pitched roof, making it extremely hot and clammy... haha), the jacuzzi with its funky blue lights, the cool wine cellar with the beer dispenser / pressure thingy, and the courtyard, etc.

A lot of bareback porn fun with all the twinky boys, hehe. Today I'm going to see if I can try to explore the local area around the house. There is a small lake close by and a little village; maybe I could pick up some lost country boy, hehe, and bring him back to the house for some fun or even 'rape' him in a bush somewhere, naughty hehe.

Anyhow, till next time, enjoy the pictures from my countryside adventure on my blog. (I even made a short little video you can see there).

Hugs - Anton

Readers online comments:

I - naughty boys...

II - sounds like horny fun indeed

WEEK XV

BORTA BRA MEN HEMMA BÄST

Hey all. I spent most of this week in Prague and the Czech countryside, as you know if you read my previous blog post. It was a very exciting and also relaxing week, enjoying the steaming sun, watching the little, cute birds getting fed by their mum (although we found a dead bird on the doorstep on the day we left; hope it wasn't mama bird).

The day we went in to the Prague centre with the boys, most of the guys spent the time chasing souvenirs and watching a 600 year old clock ticking by - but you should know me well enough by now to know that would never be a complete day for me, hehe.

After flirting with the cute waiter in a gay-friendly cafe, I learnt that there was free internet there so I got on Grindr straight away. Half an hour later I was picked up by a local hotty escort and sexy horny bareback guy. It turned out he was a big fan of mine who had all my TIM movies; he's a huge fan of TIM stuff, so it was pretty cool to meet him. Honestly, I never think there are people who are fans of mine; it's just strange to think of it in that way - I mean, I'm just little old me, after all.

Anyhow, back at his place we quickly got naked and, after a brief shower, jumped in bed together, where I enjoyed his horny bum and he enjoyed my rock hard cock. After rimming him good I shot a huge load in his hole. He cleaned my cock with his mouth and gave me a nice massage; he also tried to fuck me but I was too tight (need to practice, lol). We chilled a bit before he dropped me back at the central plaza, where I introduced him to the other jealous lads, hehe. I love Prague. It's so pretty, with the big castle overshadowing the old town and the river.

But all good things must come to an end, and so we finally left. After a 26 hour drive with a trailer behind us, and getting stopped by a handsome German police officer named

Stefan at border control (who let us go when he saw the camera equipment in the trunk, laughing at us giving him the coy eye), we finally reached London. Tired but happy. I have two American guys and a British guy staying for a few days in the flat, as the hubby is away in LA. They are sticking around a bit, enjoying the London life for a bit before they are returning home to the US.

Yesterday my good friend, a Greek/German guy who's a sexy photographer, popped over to check them out (always nice, hehe). On my first day back in the architect office, I just couldn't help it - I was soooo horny - I invited a local guy to the office toilet, where I sucked his big cock and he deep-throated me. He shot a nice, big load deep in my throat and wiped it in my beard, then zipped up and left me wanting more, hehe.

A couple of hours later I invited over another lad who just wanted to suck me, and I mouth-fucked him so hard against the wall I thought I would shoot my big load into the cubicle next door, hehe. He certainly knew how to deep-throat a big cock and made me cum so much.

Just before leaving work, another hot lad texted me. I thought to myself, should I? And before I could answer my thought, my cock had already texted back: 'see u soon'. Five minutes later he came over, a very fit lad, and I gave him a load in his bum as he eagerly bent over, waiting for my cream.

Wow, what a day, such a whore haha! It's so nice to be back; as they say in Swedish, "borta bra men hemma bäst" (it's good to be away, but it's best to come home, or there is no place like home, I guess).

Tuesday was a bit similar: drawing windows, lunch break, blowjob in the toilets, drawing door frames, another office toilet blowjob, more window drawings, hehe. Wednesday was a bit calmer, just had a blowjob in an eye hospital (only because they have good private toilets there, lol) with a hot lad I met in the local cruising toilet. After work I met an old friend who runs a porn site and who needed help with some drawings. We got talking about porn and what it means nowadays, when it's so easily available to everyone (most everyone, anyhow). Interesting thoughts. Anyhow, that's all for this week.

Hugs from London
Anton

Readers online comments:

I - Anton looks so sexy in the picture he took of himself with his shirt up, but completely different in the other ones...

II - what, no stories about a pit stop at the baths?! weak!

III - Hehe the mysteries with photos... Hehe, different days different beards lol

WEEK XVI

SLUT (noun)

Hey, guys. This week I was chatting with a guy and had a very interesting conversation, where he basically told me he hadn't slept with anyone for over 6 months. It became clear that one of the major reasons it had been so long was that he felt he was not so attractive - although to me (and I'm sure most others) he looked very hot, indeed. Anyhow, the discussion got a bit heated, as can sometimes happen when chatting online (which I'm sure you all know, hehe) and he called me a slut, amongst other things, for having sex with three guys in one day etc.

In fairness, it made me chuckle to myself a bit - if someone wants to insult me, they'll have to come up with something better than that! But then it got me thinking, what does "being a slut" mean? So I started thinking about the definition of "slut". Is it having a lot of sexual partners? Fucking anonymously? Not having a steady partner, or maybe having one whilst engaging with others? This led to thoughts of what sex is and why we humans do it. I think it's the last resort of our animalistic side trying to express itself, our raw, inner raging stallions, bursting with hormones, trying to escape.

That brought me to my little conclusion that, as being a slut, I'm basically very bad at inhibiting my inner animal rawness, or I'm easily seduced by the horny stallion inside me (or, even better, the one releasing a load or two in a sexy bum boy, hehe). Anyhow, that made me smile to myself on the bus into work, and I like smiling.

To celebrate that I'm a slut, I invited the hot guy I met in the eye clinic over to my office toilet, where I fucked his eager mouth till I came good and deep in it; he is such an expert deepthroater. I also met my new favourite Greek/German photographer friend. We did a little nude shoot with a really hot Polish boy, a friend of a friend, for my new book (coming out later this year).

Apart from that, this week has been pretty eventless. I was

introduced to an online game by some American porn boys and I'm totally hooked, Diablo III. I'm already a Level 14 magician and my favourite spell is three fire hydras - phallic, I know, lol.

Popped in to the clinic for some tests/checkups and all is well, so I'm happy. I only wish it was more like summer here but then again, Dino is back tomorrow, which is even better than the sun. Oh, I almost forgot: it was my birthday the other day. I turned 37 on 16th July, old man me (lol)!

Big hugs from a chilly London,
Anton

Readers online comments:

I -Being in touch with your animal instincts should not make you a slut. Its more like being self-aware.

II - Being a slut is hot. I'd love to be your slut one good time. With three guys!

III - I wish I could find someone to be a fellow slut with. No judgements, just some nekkid fun. Besides it's more fun to "push the envelope" with a bud!

IV - hehe so I'm a self-aware slut, awesome hehe, yeah I love having fun with fellow slutty guys hehe, always fun

WEEK XVII

GYM BLOW BUDDIES

A friend of mine is currently looking for a gym and possibly gym buddy, and I thought I might look for something together with him. The gyms in London are very expensive so three years ago I decided to stop going; it was just getting to be too much, and I realized that the only things I was doing in the gym anyhow were 3 sets of 50 sit-ups and a few chest pumps. Than straight into the sauna, which was like a cruising paradise on my office lunchbreaks. We used to suck a lot of cock and got sucked even more, hehe, and sometimes a boy got to have my big, raw cock in his horny bum in the steamroom. It was a nice and relaxing lunch, indeed, but an expensive one I admit as the gym was like £90/month, hehe.

I guess I've been blessed with having my old ballet body, which doesn't seem to lose much of its shape, although my flexibility is totally gone nowadays (I'm happy if I can sit in a 50-90 degree 'split', hehe). As I get older, though, I'm sure that this will change and I'll start needing to look after myself more. I was never a huge fan of big muscles or over-pumped gym-bodies. Defined, yes, and a bit of lovely shape in the right places is always hot, but what really turns me on these days is self confidence in a guy. Not sure why this is, but there's something so hot about a guy who knows what he wants and just takes it. Or gives it, if that's what he wants to do hehe.

The determination in his face, the strong eyes and look, yum yum yum. This week my flatmate came back from the States. It's nice to have him back in town for a while before he heads over to LA again. We spent Saturday walking around the South Bank and Soho, watching all the guys cuming out in their short shorts, as summer has finally arrived. Then we went to the cinema; I love films as you might have guessed hehe. (You can see some photo's from our adventures around town on my blog as usual, just search in the archive section of it). Apart from that, it's been a pretty normal, quiet week - a few blowjobs here and there, horny boys in my office toilet between work on designing bathrooms, etc. Always fun, hehe. Also, I'm very excited about Liam's new DVD coming out soon, SLAMMED. He showed me the initial edits for the trailer - can't wait to see the final version of it! I'm sure you will love it.

Next week I'll talk about "the second coming out", so brace yourselves! Only kidding, hehe; it will be interesting, hopefully.

Have a good week.
hugs Anton

Readers online comments:

I - Hugs

II - nice post Anton.... I can relate to the ex dancer body comments.... my flexibility is shit now too but I think I may have over extended in other ways than on stage:) Also really looking forward to Slammed... the pre-release scene was great.

III - Success Anton! :)

IV - Hehe cool Yeah the slammed DVD is looking to be one HOTTTTTTT thing, I think one of Liam's best ones tbh hehe and that's saying a lot...!

V - INDEED!

WEEK   XVIII

I LIKE the Z in poZ

"Oh so controversial..." No, not really: this week I'll be talking about "the second cuming out", as I believe Director/Producer Paul Morris (TIM) so correctly labeled it. And that is coming out as poz, i.e. as an HIV positive man. The weird thing about HIV, to me, was always the "shame" factor - that someone who caught it mostly felt. Or that somehow they were supposed to feel ashamed of themselves. Set aside from society in a way, and made to feel less of a person. I never quite understood this, as to me it was always "just another disease". (After all does a smoker feel ashamed for smoking and catching lung-cancer?)

Although it has taken me many years to come to terms with my own status, and to be totally honest with myself and others. The other day, for example, I was talking to an old friend I haven't heard from in many years, and it turns out that he had been very ill. He'd been bitten by a foreign mosquito when travelling abroad and, eight years later, suffered the terrifying consequences badly. I don't want to go into the details too much but it sounded a right ordeal. My first reaction was, of course, how sad and scary, and how lucky the doctors found out in time, and that he got the treatment in time to safe his life.

Not for one second did I think, "Hmm, he should have been more careful when going abroad", or "he shouldn't have gone abroad", etc. I know the circumstances and things like the risk factors are completely different, but my point is that, rather than casting blame, we should show moral and physical support, etc. Not just from health clinics but society as a whole. Just my thoughts on the subject.

Anyhow, don't be afraid to cum out. It's like in Harry Potter: the more people afraid of mentioning Voldemort's name, the scarier and stronger he becomes, right? There is a world in the future where HIV will be considered just another deadly disease - one not over-shadowed by secrecy and silence, and superstition and moral dilemmas. So let's get over the HIV stigma and get there already. The only way to do this, I think, is by honesty and pride, not shame and closed closet doors. I'm bored of hidden code words and "testing the waters" in chat rooms etc, trying to find other poz lads to bareback fuck with.

Apart from that, I have of course, been a very naughty man lately. I went to a local gay sauna with my best friend, and I quickly disappeared into the dark rooms that have glory hole cubicles, where I lent out my cock to different horny men's bums and faces, one after the other. I must have shot at least 4 loads that evening in a couple of hours.

Also today I had two horny lads popping by my office and dumping their juicy loads in my mouth before heading back to their work desks, while I went back to my desk, realizing I still had a bit of sticky cum in my beard, blush. I stank of sex and cum; the young intern on my left side must have smelt it, hehe.

Next week I'll be writing about another biggy: love and relationships, or at least what it means to me (if anyone cares to listen.) I loveeeee hugs, and I steel hugs from most people I run into.

Hugs anton

Readers online comments:

I - There will always be those straight and gay ignorant assholes out there that do not understand a fucking thing and act
out on their ignorance. Knowledge is tolerance.

> I a - Indeed, unfortunately so. And more gay ones
> than straight ones sometimes lol

II - I was just diagnosed this spring. It was a shock after two
decades of bb sex, but the stigma and shame were unexpected.
I kind of feel stupid, but, it comes with the territory when
you are a cum whore bottom and love anonymous sex with as
many men as you can get. And I do.

> IIa - Yeah but stigma can be beaten, we need to unite
> and be strong, and it will die down with time I be-
> lieve! Do eat your daily two Brazil nuts per day (no
> more than 3) it will help your selenium values up
> which will help your immune system fight the virus
> and increase your cd4 counts

III - hugz

IV - and a little squeeze...

V - I totally agree with you. People need to stop playing the
judgmental blame game crap when it comes to those who are
poz.

VI - The "stigma" is the after-effect of the once understandable idea, a generation back, of reconsidering whether some
mens' overt sexual behavior got them this disease; and there's
little denying that many, who "fucked around," got it that way.
But it wasn't the rampant sex that created the epidemic, it was
the lack of understanding or treatment. In the years hence, the
establishments - and "established notions" - of the health (and
"gay culture") groups that came about at that time, who suc-
cessfully mis-used the idea of reversing our sexual course as

a way to gain a foothold and sympathy - which then morphed into even more ideologies of praising those who'd turn their natural sexual impulses to more traditional-minded ways - nowadays find it impossible to espouse a different course when it cums to male intercourse. Because, to be blunt, it fucks up their entire business model. Getting the "powers-that-be" to change their position - from the "fear of a death sentence" to that of dealing with a quite livable condition? Yeah, only if to them it makes "dollars and sense" to them first. Meanwhile, Anton, you hottie, I'd be honoured if I were ever in a position/ place to have you fuck the beJesus outta me, and your nut in my barefuckin' porn arse!

> VIa - Thank u so much for those words, u are a beautiful soul! And if be honoured to fuck u mate, real manly pleasures to be shared
> VIb - I think you're a beautiful soul too. Along with being an articulate, thoughtful, and importantly provocative one at that ! Plus, the more you (and I) bring our manly/sexual motivations out in the open, the more others will question there's. Which is a healthier out CUM for all men. Speaking of CUM (LOL), I do think when guys fuck under naturally raw (unadulterated and unfettered) conditions it's as mas culine as it gets. So yeah, if we two were ever to fuck (and let's hope so, handsome !), the manly pleasures will be tenfold indeed !

VII - Thanks for the hugs and feedback, much appreciated, And fucking is like a second or even first instinct to me hehe Can't get enough of it lol, blush

> VIIa - Aint that the truth ! Men like us fuck outta pure insatiable instinct ; yet so many other gay men, who have the same natural sexual hungers, would rather deny that about themselves and behave in a more disciplined manner (at least publicly) in order to gain the favor of the traditional mainstream ! BTW, anytime - and any place - hung and handsome ! XXX

VIII - How exactly do 'honesty' and 'pride' fit with having bb sex with multiple guys in sauna glory holes? You disclose every time? The boys you fuck are all poz already? I totally agree that the shame and stigma should be removed from hiv, but behaviour can be shameful and if you're as irresponsible as it seems you deserve all the stigma you get.

> VIIIa - Most people I fuck with do indeed know my status, they either seen my films and cum to that conclusion by themselves, or it's is revealed in conversations by chatting online etc. I don't go to sex clubs / etc that often tbh, and most of my sexual activities consists of blowjobs. But my point is that ANY sexually active person shares an equally important part of protecting themselves. It has shown on tests that apparently poz men thinks that if a partner is not insisting on protection he presumes the other one is poz too. Equally the study showed that if the guy was negative and his partner didn't insist on protection he presumes that the other one is negative. I think the route to the problem is this: EQUAL responsibility is the key. It's not a blame game, it's not an evil act, sex is fun, and yes we should protect the people we are with, as far as it's possible, ofcourse. I never blamed the person I got poz by, cause what's the point in that? It's not a question of Who's fault it is or Why? It's a question of how we do to move on from here, how do we make things better, and I was equally as responsible as he was to me becoming poz...

IX - The second cumming out leads to the end of the shame which was never there in the first place.

> IXa - There are still people that feel ashamed at that they became positive, It's so strange I find it, these things happen, I mean does a lung cancer patient feel shame / guilt for smoking and getting sick that way?

X - Very interesting article. I agreed with the first part but I found the second part possibly irresponsible. If you didn't disclose your status to those people you were fucking, I think it is wrong.

> Xa - I disclose my status as often as I can, depending on the circumstances
>
> Xb - I had the toxic sign tattooed on my body. I ask my fuck buddies if they have seen it and know what it means. Once that is out of the way, and under stood, we can get down to good old BB. Hugs
>
> Xc - That's a good idea, if only I wasn't so afraid Of needles... Hugs anton
>
> Xd - Nothing to it, Anton. You soon get used to the needle. I really like tattoos, on myself and other guys. Would love to see a few on you. Hugs. Daniel.

XI - very interesting, and can't wait till your next article. I love hugs to :)

XII - I understand perfectly Anton. I practice bb and I love it. Cumming in a guy ass or cumming inside me or swallowing or to be swallowed are for me the most intense pleasure.

XIII - After all that you said, you're going to make me wood more !

XIV - Fucking in random gloryholes? SIMPLY DISGUSTING

> XIVa - Hehe obviously someone is missing out on something... Mr grumpy wood lol

CHRONICLES OF A LONDON CUMPIG

WEEK XIX

LOVE & SEX

Hi, guys. Hope you all had a wonderful week. I would like to thank you all for the poZitive response I had to the last weeks blog post - much appreciated, big hugZ. As promised, this week I'm biting the bullet on yet another biggy: love and sex, and how they go alongside each other, although maybe not always as predictable as what is the normally anticipated ways of life. As you probably figured out by now I'm a bit of a tinker (that's "Irish" for thinker, as an ex bf taught me, hehe), and these weekly blog writings have been really good for me, as a way of gathering my thoughts, which don't always come in the correct order. (I was in a German porn scene a long time ago. It was a group scene and the director was screaming madly at all of us in broken English, as apparently we came in the wrong order, hehe.)

So, LOVE: What is it? I've been in love three times in my life. The first one was fifteen years ago. That's a long time ago and I'm still not over it; what a hopeless romantic I am. We dated for five years, after which we kinda grew apart from each other sexually and became good friends instead, like brothers, a purely platonic relationship. London is an expensive town so we kept living together. It was hard at first but we grew accustomed to it.

A couple of years later, while still living together, we were both dating different guys and at the same time doing porn on the side. By now some of you might have figured out who this is (hehe). My second and third boyfriends, although they were really nice guys and the sex was great, I couldn't quite connect with them as I'd done with my first one. It just wasn't the same and I felt I was being unfair towards them both in many ways, comparing them with my ex in so many ways. They also found it a bit difficult, which is totally understandable as my living arrangements were the same as before.

However my current situation, in many ways, I see as ideal. I live with my first love and we are the very best of friends in the world, soulmates and life partners in so many ways (apart from in the bedroom haha). And although we share the same amazingly big and beautiful bed, there is no hanky panky and there isn't any need or desire from either of us for it. We know we are there for one another, emotionally, financially and in any other ways - just not sexually. It's a purely platonic relationship. We can than have sex with who-ever we want, whenever we want; I seem to have a bit of a higher sex drive though, lol (if you haven't realized this by now). And there are no jealousy issues whatsoever. It's the best of both worlds.

We gay men live such strangely different lives from our straight counterparts. We have the freedom to make up our worlds as we go along, and the way we create our relation-ships with our friends and lovers, etc. it's truly amazing. We should really take advantage of this, I think, as long as you are open with one another and say what you feel honestly. That's the best way forward because secrets create hard feelings and bad relations etc.

Love is in the air but lust is, too. They don't always go together. It's like in ancient Greece, where they had two words for love (or even more if you look into it further): AGAPE for strong brotherly (platonic) love, and EROS for lustful love. This reminds me to mention I'm working on a little short film called "agapEros", which is a short reflection of these thoughts and my life, in a way, the combination of the two loves. I'm hoping that it will be accepted for screening at the Berlin Porn Film Festival this October (fingers crossed). It features scenes shot on the hot Newport beach in the States, as well as footage of a few scenes from Treasure Island Me-dia, with special permission from Paul Morris ofcourse (many thanks!).

Apart from that, this week has been kinda quiet. Dino went back to LA to direct some stuff over there and I miss him very much, as usual. But me and Liam are already planning our trip to Berlin for the Porn Film Festival and hopefully to film a few hot scenes for Treasure Island Media, so I'm looking forward to that, will be a lot of fun indeed.

Oh, and I got two loads in my mouth in the office toilets today. When I sat down between two young interns, I noticed cum in my beard; no doubt I stank of sex, blush, lol. I went to see two naughty, hot muscle guys on Saturday. They'd been up playing all night so they were a bit tired, bless, but I shot two loads in one of their bums. Also had my hot photographer friend pop over to do a photoshoot in the basement, but the fun really began when the model left hehe.

Hugs anton

Readers online comments:

I - I think you are my brother:)

II - only a brother I'd wanna fuck around with:)

III - Hehe would be lots of fun for sure sexy hehe

IV - I completely hear you on this. I live with my ex. We were together for 10 years but life threw us a whole bunch of curveballs in a very short time. The relationship died because of it and yet, we still share a bed, our hearts and our lives. We snuggle, care for each other and yet, no hanky panky. We call it a "companionship". And it works for us. PS Do you or "D" like tubby Aussie guys with no gag reflex :) ?? PS love your writings Sir. Very articulate and thoughtful. Shalom and blessings.

V - It has taken me a million broken hearts to get a good understanding of the difference between a fuck and sex with someone you love. Hoping with age that things will make more sense.

WEEK XX

THE REVENGE FUCK

Hi, horny fuckers (hehe). This week is a bit of a follow up on last week's blog entry, dealing with the cheating aspect of relationships. As I've learnt over the years - not only from personal experience - most relationships have them. At one point or another, there is that little unspoken fuck in the toilets at a club while the bf was out of town. Or the blowjob in a sauna at the gym when no one was watching etc...

It's all fine, guys, but I think it's important to be honest with your partner about them. This is how I dealt with one such experience in the past (maybe not so admirable but it was fun to plan and execute, hehe): I had an Irish bf who I knew was cheating on me. When I confronted him about it and asked him to come clean with me, assuring him I wouldn't be upset, he just couldn't do it. (No doubt this was caused by modern society's pressure on how we should think and act in terms of monogamy etc... blah blah blah.)

Anyhow, I decided to set a trap; knowing my ex, I had to make it an elaborate one. So I created a fake online profile on Gaydar with some hot pics of a sexy guy I knew he would like (not too hot though, since it had to be believable at the same time), and started messaging him from it. At the same time I told my ex I was going to Sweden. He saw me book the tickets but I told him I was leaving a day before I actually was.

While my online alter-ego was arranging a fuck with my ex at his place, I was on the phone with him saying bye while he wished me a safe journey. I finished off my online chat telling him to make sure he was well lubed up, to leave the door open and be on his bed face-down, which he thought was a horny idea. When I made my way over to his place, his door was indeed open, such an obedient boy hehe...

I sneaked into the bedroom, where he was lying face down, ass up, his bum cheeks spread wide open for me. Without saying a word, I ripped of my trackies (I was bare-chested as it was a hot day). I was going commando for easy cock access and was hard in a tick. I mounted on top of him quickly, forcing my throbbing cock into his juicy boy hole. I pressed his head into the pillow when he tried to turn around to face me. Then, as I shot a huge load into his arse, I said, "So, Mr. Cheater, having a good day so far?"...

The speed with which he turned around to face me was incredible, and the look on his face - god, it was amazing, lol, priceless. I've never seen such a guilty, but yet just totally pleasured face. Priceless!!! I noticed that the sheets below him were all wet with cum, so he had clearly enjoyed the fuck too. The first thing he said, believe it or not, was, "I knew it was you all along"... As if, haha.. That face betrayed him.

Anyhow, we sat down and had a long talk, and again I explained to him I'm not like other stereotypical boys with jealousy issues. I can understand the manly needs of feeling horny and wanting variety; that's all natural and what it is like being a man. The most important thing for me, though, is honesty between two guys. That's gold, and now that was broken...

On another note, I had another boyfriend ones, "popping out to see his sister" here in London at 11PM after chatting on Gaydar all evening... Please, can we make it more obvious? Oh yes, hang on - half an hour later, his sister called, from Greece... Oh dear, honesty always wins, trust me.

Horny at work now, need a lubed up boy to fuck, yeah baby.
Hugs, Anton

Readers online comments:

I - At least you got a hot fuck. I hate getting caught, or out smarted, but I would have had the most delicious feeling of contempt for you as well as utter admiration that I had just been fucked by you because you out witted me. That is hot. So is your dick.

> Ia - Hehe thanks mate, and yeah no one wants to get caught So honesty should prevail... thank u, blushes

II - That moment when he turned around and saw you must have been such a head-fuck for him!

> IIa - Hehe yeah he was very perplexed hehe and satisfied and shocked and guilty etc all at ones... I remember that face clearly hehe

III - Fuck that sounds so hot. I would love to be on all fours waiting for you Anton. Hopefully pre-lubed with a different guys load.

IV - Great story. I take it. It was before camera phones cause seeing his face when he turned around would have been priceless.

> IVa - Hehe I know right, No unfortunately I had a shitty phone at the time hehe Damn... Hehe

V - Would love to be there as well

VI - Nice read! Haha... People always find out one way or another but your online trick was really good! Lol

VII - My ex was exactly the same. "Went to hang out with a mate" at 11pm, when we were half way through watching a film. Riiiiight. The irony was it was an open relationship and I was always honest about when I was going to hook up with someone, but he just would never tell me when he did. Gays. What a bunch of fags. :P

VIII - I love being tied and ready, door unlocked and gagged.

IX - Cheating implies that you don't know what is going on... However you knew what he was doing? Is it really necessary to say that you fucked a twink last night? Your bf prob knows and doesn't need the visual memory. Also, if your both pos, think about re-infecting your partner with other STDs, so if your fucking other people get tested often. Finally, I do think you can be monogamous, not because of societal pressure but because only your BF can satisfy you. It's a powerful feeling knowing that only one person hits the spot! If you need others maybe you should just be fuck buddies for example?

X - LOVED this post! I AM a firm believer in honesty, and it is a shame that there is not enough of it in the world. And as someone who is quite good at avoiding people that are jealous, I AM happy to hear that you are not a jealous guy. Kudos to you! And I would have LOVED to have seen the face of your boyfriend when he turned around!!

CHRONICLES OF A LONDON CUMPIG

WEEK   XXI

WATCHING PORN

I remember the first time I watched porn - I must have been around 11 or 12. Being 37 now, that was a long time ago, hehe. I say "porn" but it was just a magazine. An old, dirty, and torn porn magazine that a friend and I found in a play nest some kids had built in the nearby forest, close to where I lived in the north of Sweden.

My friend, who was a year older than me, told me older kids used to go there for "fun, naughty times together". He sounded like he knew what he was talking about but I don't think he actually had a clue either haha. I remember how strange I thought it was, but at the same time appealing and pleasurable. Watching those bearded men with their hairy chests and massive cocks forcing them into the colourfully dressed and undressed 80's hairstyled women, and the settings... oh the lovely settings, so kitch and camp and seedy all at ones haha. I returned there a few more times, alone in the evening with a torch, and I remember comparing my tiny cock with the guys in the photos and hoping mine would grow as big one day, hehe. Did it, I wonder? lol.

Can you then believe the joy and wonder when I discovered a similar magazine, this one whole and with no torn-out pages, in my mums bottom wardrobe box! It was well hidden away and, I think, must have been a remnant of her brief marriage, he was a bit of a naughty man... I took it out of its mini thin box, an old soap box from a foreign country. That gave the magazine a sweet flowery smell, and made the pervy experience when unfolding the pages and looking at the glorious uncut cocks playing in their female counterparts even more pleasurable.

I used my mum's carpeted floor as friction to create magic in my pants while turning page after page. Those magic moments when mum was away from home, hehe, ooh la la. I was always envious of the guys in the photos. They seemed so focussed and so content. I didn't understand it, but I liked it a LOT, and I knew one day that would be me (well, sort of, anyhow). I wonder how it is nowadays growing up, when porn is so much more widely available. Back then it could be weeks and even months between sessions of sneaking out into the forest or playing on the carpet - oh, the anticipation, the frustration, lol. Life is so much faster nowadays, and there are so much things that fights for our attention and limited time.

This week has been a quiet one for me. I've been playing an online game (Diablo III) like a proper nerd - I'm a level 52 wizard now in HELL mode, where I'm beating down demons by the minute. Oh and I've started talking to a handsome homeless person on my way back home from work every day.

More about that in another blog.
Hugs anton

Readers online comments:

I - It's true, there was such a mystery to growing up and only seeing a glimpse or two of sex at a time. Some magic must be lost. As a child of the 90s, I remember getting my first peak at hardcore porn videos through the noise of a pay-per-view channel. That accidental partial unscramble brought me such excitement! Ahh memories. Kids today are assholes anyway though. Fuck em.

II - A handsome homeless man, huh? I want to read that blog post! I remember once having picked up a hot latino who spoke no English. Turned out he was a migrant orange picker. He was one HOT fuck! I love a big uncut cock and when they are hard, language is irrelevant. lol

III - Oh sounds exciting, scrambled channels

WEEK   XXII

CONTRAST LIFE

"If we can help one other person in this life, we have justified our own existence." I just sat down next to a cute, Russian, homeless young guy (25 years old) by the Tube station today and had a very long discussion. He told me the story of how he became homeless. He's been in the UK for 5 years, the last two of which he's been living on the streets. It started when he lost control of his alcohol and drug problem. From there things went very fast: He lost his job, his flat, his friends turned their backs on him, and he found out he had hep C, which caused him depression and made him drink even more.

Despite all this he came across as a very bright young man, who just hadn't been that lucky in life. I gave him my card and said if he wanted I could try to help him get back on his feet again, maybe I could help him find some counseling help, and offered him someone he could call to if he was in serious trouble. When I asked where he slept, he laughed and said it depended on whether he'd had a good day, as the beds at the homeless shelters cost £12-14; otherwise he slept in a garage entrance or anywhere safe-ish he could find.

I just find it so sad and crazy that in the year 2012, in the western civilized world, there isn't a better system in place. We take our blissful, blessed lives for granted, thanking our lucky stars, wishing we could do more to help those less fortunate - but at the same time not doing much. Sorry for dampening your day. It just got me really sad, so I decided to paint this weekend; that's usually how I try to deal with tricky emotional things, to get them out of my system.

Apart from that my week has been very busy. The architect boss is away so I've been managing affairs and supervising things as much as possible, which is always fun. I mouth fucked a few horny boys in the office toilets, which I enjoy. But the most HORNY part was that I did a very sexy shoot for Liam Cole in an empty garage in south London, with a hot American bottom boy (Luke Bennett) and a sexy, hung top Sebastian Slater. We first met up in a local pub and wandered over to the garage (later I found out it was broken into hehe), where, as soon as the doors closed, we were all over the boy, fucking his mouth and bum hard and rough, hehe. He is truly a stunningly hot and greedy bottom lad, with absolutely no gag reflex - something I know how to appreciate, hehe. I came so much and pushed it into his greedy boy hole and got him to clean up my cock after, with his mouth ofcourse...

While walking back from the tube to my flat (wearing trackies and no underpants), a young guy caught my eyes and with one look I knew he was going to follow me into the back alley behind Tesco (a food shop close to my flat). As soon as we entered a dark area, he was down on his knees, pulling out my already hard cock and started to deepthroat it big time. He was very talented orally also, hehe.

I pulled him up and dived down on his nice cut cock, and after a very short time he came all over my beard; licking his balls, I smeared his cum all over his cock and my face. It was so hot, double wham.

So many mixed emotions, how is a man to deal with all this? We just try our best, in all different ways.

Big naughty hugs Anton

Readers online comments:

I - There's a really interesting chapter on solving homelessness by Malcolm Gladwell in, I think it's "What the dog saw" but it might be "The Tipping Point". Both books are interesting reads Anton; you might like them. Also, those boys were so lucky; I'd love to be gagging on your cock :D

II - The journey from functional and self providing to homeless and destitute can be surprisingly short. I hope he calls and takes up your offer of assistance. Nice thing you did.

III - I saw him a few month later (after I hadn't seen him around for a month or so), this time he was wearing almost clean clothes, and he was with a young woman, and what looked like their young daughter, the woman seemed bossy, and he seemed to be happier. Maybe he managed to clean up a bit and got back together with his wife or something. He seemed busy and I didn't want to interrupt. Hugs a

WEEK XXIII

SLAMMED

Hey, horny fuckers. This week I'm writing about my experience with the latest Liam Cole film, SLAMMED. The trailer for SLAMMED went online a couple of weeks ago and has provoked strong reaction, both negative and positive. I find it extremely interesting that people feel so strongly about porn and I'm happy to read all the different comments; after all, we're all individuals and are entitled to our own points of view. My personal view of it is that good porn often pushes boundaries. I don't mind criticism of the porn I participate in, I don't take personal offense, - I just give them a virtual hug, hehe.

For example, in response to The Sword's piece on SLAMMED, I posted the jokey comment about "Unsafe sex - is it safe?" The replies to that comment were very strong, but some rather funny, I have to admit. Among other things, two people commented saying that I'm personally "human scum." I think it's interesting they got so angry as to attack like that. I'd rather eat their cum, lol, but never mind that - one can only laugh at ignorance, I think.

Porn has always been a medium for voyeuristic exhibitionistic behaviours and desires. The reasons people do and don't enjoy watching it has always fascinated me and, in a way, that's why I decided to get into it in the first place. There's all sorts of porn that people find enjoyable to watch, featuring all sorts of desires and fetishes - bareback sex, condom sex, gay, lesbian, bi, and straight, animal sex, domination sex, fisting sex, sleeping sex (where people are being given "sedatives" and "raped") and so on and so forth...

Some porn movies are about fantasies, such as devil and angel sex; some are based on famous mainstream films, like The Hole; and some are realistic, hot 'n' horny man-on-man action, like the Treasure Island Media DVD's. But they do share one thing in common: an underlying sexuality and our eagerness to watch and to be watched while doing naughty things - things we are not meant to be doing and not meant to be enjoying, and god forbid being "seen doing", but we still do them and we still enjoy them. For example, who hasn't tried to hide or cover themselves up while wanking when someone unexpectedly walks into the room, when you thought no one was home? Why is this? Because it's "forbidden" to wank openly in our modern society. It's the biggest and worst-kept secret in the universe: we all masturbate and if we don't, we bloody well should (it would make a lot of people happier in the office, I tell you, hehe).

My point is this: I don't watch much lesbian porn, as it doesn't make me horny and it doesn't give me pleasure or satisfaction, so I don't feel naughty. And I want to feel naughty. I want to feel a bit guilty. In a way you create a story in your head while watching porn, don't you? Pushing your own boundaries of what is acceptable a bit further each time, searching new adventures in your mind, testing the ground. I say if you find something horny to watch, than watch it; and if you don't want to, then don't. Can't be more simple than that.

On that note, go and buy Liam Cole's new DVD SLAMMED, for no other reason than that I'm in a really hot duo scene hehe! And I'm not high on anything, just fucking horny, as usual. Do I wonder if the other guys are high or not? No, I don't. I just love to fuck bareback, that's it. Seriously though, it's a really hot fuck feast. I've seen parts of it and really can't wait to get myself a copy, hehe! Apart from that I had a fun shoot this week. Not porn but clothes promotion for a Chinese company with my awesome photographer friend Claudio. I popped a T.I.M. vest on him and he loved it, so I took some hot pics of him. Now that I've given mine away, I might have to beg Paul for another one, hehe.

Big naughty hugs – Anton

Readers online comments:

I - You dudes are far more brill than I realized

II - Well said Anton, I could not agree more. Don't like it then don't watch it. But there are these condom nazi's who want to go further and ban it. They all should move to North Korea or something.

III - Wonderful scene, thanks for sharing! Look after yourself lovely man ;)

IV - This is from a smart man who understands the human condition and thrives in it.

V - Love this scene... Jake was my screen saver for a while :P
        Va - Hehe yeah I bet, he was one fucking horny sexy pig bottom. Loved it

VI - The way I see it is; it's all natural, meant to be, we are "human animals" separating us from the "non-human animals". Piggy... any rancher knows that a well trained pig is the cleanest animal around... same goes for filth... Just words to demean something that is totally natural... ever take time to look at two studs connected together in a fuck, we fit together like a jigsaw puzzle... amazing when you think about it, and yes fucking NATURAL since man walks upright... Homo Erectus and not Man with hardon... So to use those words to excite the mind and mock those who used them for whatever reason, we sex our brains off.

VII - Funny... the kissing is what got me rock hard to.... Well that and the chem... but Jon & Keiran were SO passionate... Totally wanted to b there!!!

VIII - I love hearing about Anton's scenes! Please keep them coming.

IX - I think some people will love it and others will find it disturbing. But that could be said of a lot of TIM's stuff over the years.

X - I am so grateful to Jon and Keiran for that night. For me, the intensity of this SLAMMED clip is what making porn is all about.

XI - cool! I bet its going to be very very good!

XII - Jon Phelps is fucking gorgeous!

XIII - This video was so hot and would of love to be there.

XIV - Slammed in more ways than one by the looks of this...

XV - Wow, fucking hot scene! That guy is so slammed! Wish it was me in his place!

CHRONICLES OF A LONDON CUMPIG

WEEK XXIV

POUNDING HIM GOOD

Hey, horny guys. Hope you all have been enjoying Liam Cole's latest DVD Slammed. I haven't got my copy yet but am awaiting it eagerly, hehe. This week has been kinda quiet. I've had a few photo shoots, one with my hot friend Claudio,where I got to wear the TIM top with the dick man (designed by Liam Cole).

I also put together two different calendars with some of the twinky male models I've been photographing over the last year. I hope you guys like them; you can see them in the shop section on my webpage. Apart from that, it seems like Big Brother has been watching me: I got deleted from Grindr. As much as I love Apple products and the Mac brand (I'm one of those geeks who's always had Macs, ever since the first small black and white screens with only one floppy drive). But I'm not too big a fan of Apple trying to oversee every app and making everything so "protected"—it's annoying. I only put that I was looking for big cocks to film for an art project. What's offensive in that, lol? Maybe I'm being too Swedish...

This meant that I had to find other means to satisfy my big horny cock, hehe, so I went to the local park. I wasn't there long before a horny, petit, young Indian lad (24 years old, it turned out) walked in and nodded towards a cubicle. I followed eagerly and found the boy had already pulled down his pants and was bending over. His bumhole was already lubed up when I felt it, too. Wow, here was a boy who really knew what he wanted - I like that! I turned him around and pushed him down to his knees to suck my throbbing cock. As I did so I closed the door behind me and, at the same time, two eager heads belonging to two older gentlemen popped over the cubicle edge on either side to watch the boy gagging on my cock.

He stood up, turned around and pushed his bum to-wards my cock a bit too quickly, and my cock went all the way into his slim little bum. I could see the sharp pain in his face when he turned around to kiss me, but he kept it in until his bum got used to it and I could start pounding him good. I fucked him so hard and shot a big load into his hole. While he was pulling himself off, I licked my juicy cum out of his arse and then kissed him. It was fucking horny. Just a shame no one was there filming it, not even the older gentlemen in the next door cubicles ahhh. At least I can write about it now. I wonder what other action those toilets have seen? We should install cameras, hehe.

Today on my way home from work I also met my homeless friend. He's been ill recently and couldn't come out. I said he should come over one evening or weekend and I'll give him some clothes, etc. I really hope he will, and I hope he understand that I'm sincere. I wish I could do more, and at the same time I don't want to seem weird or overly pushy.

Oh, and this week my dad will be visiting from Sweden - so I have to try to behave! We'll see how that goes, hehe. Have a good one, till next week.

Big Hugs – Anton

Readers online comments:

I - You genuinely blow my mind... you just do... and that's a good thing.

WEEK   XXV

RIMMING, BLOW JOBS & DANCING

Ooh la la... I'm writing this blog post still half groggy from only sleeping 4 hours after coming back home from an awesome club night: XXL London, hehe - what a night! The evening started when a photographer friend popped round to borrow a pair of shorts for going to a club. I got curious as I hadn't been out for well over a year (I know, guys; I just had too much of the good stuff last summer and needed a break from it all, lol). So although my dad is visiting, I decided to join him and his friends.

We left home at midnight and as soon as we entered the club we knew we were in for a treat - the music on the two main dance floors and the lounge areas were great! I was wearing my skimpy, red mini-shorts; long white socks pulled up to my knees; a white T.I.M. vest, and some leather bands on my left arm and wrist. We made our way to the overcrowded dance floor, where the techniques from my go-go dance days served me well and we seemed to make quite a stir around us, hehe.

After a bit I sneaked of into the dark room. I couldn't help myself; I felt like a boy in a candy shop. I found a good place to stand on a raised platform. It was pitch black and loads of bodies were moving around in front and behind of me. I pulled out my bulging cock and before I got it all out, an eager gentlemen stopped to suck it. He was good but after a few minutes I thought I better let someone else try it. So I pulled it out of his mouth with a big wet pop, and shoved it into the mouth of the guy next to him, who had been eagerly waiting his turn, and wow, he certainly knew what he was doing..!

The next half hour I spent testing out mouth after mouth, in search of the perfect blowjob, hehe. A hot guy (Spanish, I think) with a nice, hairy, muscular torso started to finger me. I generally don't go for that, but whatever he was doing back there got me even harder, and the guy who was

sucking me off was struggling to get it all in, choking and gagging on it while I mouth fucked him. The pleasure from both
being bum-fingered and cocksucked in a dark nightclub with
the music pumping loudly through my body, and a large number of people moving and squeezing around me all combined
into total ecstasy!!

Then the man behind me went down and pushed his
tongue deep up my hairy butt crack and rimmed it good. When
he came up, I felt his cock - it was nicely shaped but small-
ish. I smiled to myself and thought, 'Good, I might even be
able to take this one.' So, while still being sucked off, I poked
my bum out a bit at him, inviting him closer... It took him a
moment before he got what I wanted. Then his cock started
to press up against my hole, stretching it - bit by bit, and then
it was in, and there was the sharp, familiar but almost forgotten pain as well as instant pleasure all at once, wow. It only
took 20 or so strokes back and forth before I came, shooting
a massive load down the gob of the new guy now sucking my
cock on his knees in front of me. Kissing the Spanish guy over
my shoulder he came too. Fucking hot! I pulled up my pants,
kissed the boy goodbye and left.

Back on the dance floor we danced even more, swing-
ing our arms to the beat, checking out all the hot men. They
really came in all sizes and shapes here, a great mix of guys,
great atmosphere, no diva kind of feel (like there can often be
from the guys with "tits", hehe), which was awesome. I ran
into a few old friends and models I've photographed, as well
as some porn stars I and my hubby know, which is always fun.

After yet another trip to the dark room, where I got
dragged in by the bf of a friend for a little ménage a trois
(which ended up some sort of six-some, lol), I stumbled upstairs to the toilets - only to find a hot, young Polish boy I 'd
kissed on the dance floor horny and drunk. I pulled him into
one of the cubicles, where we passionately kissed and he went

down on my cock, deepthroating it so good, hehe. After that I travelled back home happy and exhausted.

Apart from that, this week has been kinda quiet as my dad was visiting. It was very nice to see him. Oh, and I got nominated for "Best Top" for the Berlin Hustlaball 2012 Awards. God knows what that means, though - does it mean I have a reputation I have to live up to? LOL, scary! But if you have the time to vote for me (and for T.I.M. who were nominated in several categories), please do, hehe.

Big hugs, Anton

Readers online comments:

I - I love the "cinema verite" feel of this post. Very tantalizing
    Ia - Hehe oh thank you, I love being tantalizing hehe,

II - Cum pigs are the best to mess around with!

III - Btw what's the best way to get fucked by you?!?!?
    IIIa - I love a guy in doggy in front of me, me standing over him hehe
    IIIb - so when can you doggy me?!?!? btw. I'm 26y/o, 175cm, 72kg with a nice bubbly ass and 20cm cock ;-)

IV - So, you was to get a bunch of piggy men and mess around, Anton? ;)

WEEK XXVI

RENAISSANCE MAN

Hi, folks. This week has been a bit quiet in regards to sex. I did have a hot, horny, skinny, young Indian boy over for a few cum-relieving sessions (the very same boy as in the public loo a couple of weeks ago actually, very horny boy indeed).

But mainly I've been painting. I'm a bit down, actually. The summer is over, my soulmate is not back until the end of October, and my architecture job is a bit dull (designing dog kennels, oh dear...). So to get some emotions out, I've been doing things like painting a lot and printing out a photo of my favourite model Roland for my wall.

I also started planning a music video for an artist I've done two others for. We're hoping to film this one on the 13th October, which will be a lot of fun, hehe. I've been listening constantly to an awesome Swedish group I discovered called The Knife. Dark electro pop, which I love - it brings back memories from Sweden. With me and my hot straight friend going to crazy rave parties all over the capital and surrounding landscape.

One morning, I remember, we found ourselves in a field in the middle of nowhere, having missed the last bus back to town. We found a sheltered bus stop and he lay down on it with his head in my lap (wow!). He fell asleep like a baby, I was fucking rock-hard, massaging my cock thoroughly through the pants next to his ear. Unluckily for me, though, the bus came before I did, lol.

There are so many things I want to do in life. Some people say I do many things already, but it always feels like I'm missing something, that I'm not doing enough; I want to do and experience and create and try so many things, and one lifetime just isn't enough. Sometimes I feel like I'm about to explode with sadness, other times with happiness and joy, but always there are so many things to see and do. Life is so exciting, so extraordinary, there are so many amazing people I would love to meet and to work with (Gaga is not one of them, sorry... lol).

I passed by another handsome, young, homeless person the other day. I didn't have anything on me but stopped to talk with him a bit, asked how he was doing, etc. He said he was thirsty and asked if I had some coins for him to save up for a bed for the night. I didn't but, after passing by the bus stop, I jumped off and went back to a small shop where I bought him a Ribena juice, a packet of crisps, a sandwich, and some cookies. He was very happy to see me again.

I'm editing photos tonight. I want to create beautiful things and emotions - sad is beautiful also. What for? Beauty doesn't need a purpose; it's timeless. I want to create simple pieces that can be enjoyed for a long time. Not just simple stylistic or currently controversial pieces like everyone else seems to be doing. Nowadays, to be truly unique, one has to go back to the basics and create something that one loves. Uniqueness for uniqueness sake in itself is not unique if you see how I mean.

For me, that means striving for perfected beauty in everything I try to do. I will inevitably fail, as nothing is as pure and beautiful as our mind wants it, but that's irrelevant. It's the effort and the aim that counts: the art is in the imperfections themselves. So I hope, at least, that you know that I'm not perfect. Anyhow, what shall I have for dinner? Sausages? Swedish meatballs? Oh, and I also met a clothes designer who is going to help me on some of my video projects. Awesome!

Hugs - Anton

CHRONICLES OF A LONDON CUMPIG

WEEK XXVII

STRAIGHT BOY FANTASY

Hey! Oh wow, I'm sooo horny right now, one might say sexually frustrated or sexually teased till the brink of explosion, lol! Just had an amazingly hot straight eastern European builder guy over to help me select some photos we did together a couple of weeks ago. I had suggested he emailed me the numbers of the photos he liked, for me to edit, to save him the journey and because I thought it might be awkward otherwise for him. I had teased him a lot in my previous e-mails to him, saying things like, "can I give you a massage" and "you know guys gives better BJ's than girls", etc. But he was quite stern in his replies, saying he was totally straight, but that he preferred meeting in person to select the images together.

So I have to admit I was surprised to see him on my doorstep again. After an hour of going through the photos, I offered him a massage and he surprisingly agreed. Apparently he had been lifting stone all morning. We went into the bedroom, where I told him to take off his t-shirt and he complied. Then I told him to take off his trousers. He looked a bit perplexed, so I explained it makes things easier to massage the lower back (hehe...).

After he hesitantly obliged, I told him it would probably be best if I took off my pants also, as I'd be sitting on my knees (I left my tight vest on though, so not to scare him too much, lol). He didn't complain, so I proceed, asking him if I could use oil; I was so close to saying lube, oups... but let's use that one for the next lesson...

He lay down on the bed, face down and arms above his heads, his gorgeous, muscular, smooth but slightly scarred (from hard building work) body all nice and relaxed in front of me. I started the massage, slowly rubbing the greasy massage oil into his tight muscles. Sitting close next to him, my bare leg touching his side, I was already rock hard in my tight underpants, but luckily he didn't turn around. With my big hands and thick thumbs pressing out any knots in his backs and shoulders, he breathed heavily, pain and pleasure all mixed up it seemed.

After half an hour working his upper body, back, arms, fingers, neck, and head, I moved downwards, slowly peeling down his light blue and white boxers, little by little, massaging the side of his butt cheeks. Would he stop me? Would he turn around, pull up his underwear, and punch me? I didn't know. Excited and horny but a bit worried all at ones, I continued the massage. His butt was now completely out, gorgeous, round and muscular, a bit of blond fur trickling down into his crack; I soo wanted to rim him good. He didn't say a word, nice and relaxed in a state of hypnotized mind, miles away.

Then his phone rang. I thought it must be his girl-friend, wondering where the fuck he was - it was getting late and he had already told me she was waiting for him. He didn't answer it... Putting more oil in my hands, I let my fingers slip closer and closer to his bum crack, massaging his inner thigh, all the way till I felt his hole, so pink and innocently inviting. He didn't move, transfixed. The air was getting magnetic. I could feel the forbidden excitement; I was like a virgin again, touching my first cock. I felt his hairy balls brush against my fingers as I stroked past, massaging him.

The phone rang again, and he ignored it this time too. I moved down farther, massaging his feet. I asked him if he wanted me to do his chest. He slowly turned around, pull-ing up his underwear - was that a hard on I spotted there? He quickly put his t-shirt in his lap and sat up. "Maybe next time," he said. "I have to get back to the girlfriend, but thank you so much, it was wonderful..." After he dressed, I jokingly said, "So no blowjob this time?" Hehe. He smiled shyly. "No, I'm Christian," he said, (whatever that had to do with it lol...) "and I have a girlfriend." Again I pointed out guys give better head. Smiling, he said that was probably true. I said, "Then maybe next time?" He smiled again but didn't answer. Instead he said, "Let's do a shoot in the basement next time ok." I agreed and let him go.

Then I had a HUGEEEEE fucking wank, lol. Still though, such ashame, brain-washed by religion to sexual conformity and intimidation by the masses... Apart from that I've been editing the trailer for the porn film festival that takes place in Berlin in October. It's looking good and I'm sooo excited about going!

Hugs - Anton

Readers online comments:

I - He'll be back for that suck job. He's been thinking about it ever since.

    Ia - Hehe well he's supposedly cuming over
    Wednes day evening for a photshoot, Wish me luck
    Ib - haha See? I told you so. Good luck you hot fuck.

II - Man I am jealous. I love straight guys, it just takes them a little time before they give into pleasure. Licking straight boy hole gets me off more then anything.

    IIa - Hehe yeah I know right, love to taste his salty
    hole tomorrow, fingers crossed hehe

WEEK   XXVIII

TUBE STATION COCK SUCKING

It was a normal office day today: I picked up a croissant from the bakery, got my cock sucked by a horny city boy in the tube station toilet, did a measured survey of a building, got my cock sucked off by an old dude that creamed his pants in another station toilet. He fucking loved licking my hairy balls hehe.

Then I went back to the office to draw up the survey I've just measured up, got my cock sucked of by a horny Asian guy in another tube toilet, almost got caught by the attendant as the guy meant to watch out started sucking me also, both of them taking turns on my throbbing cock, hehe. But luckily I managed to zip up my pants before getting caught, just in time by a few second this time...

Back home I watched telly, had a wank on the chaise lounge with my pervy neighbour watching me, played a bit of Diablo III and killed some monsters with some awesome magical spells. (Tried the Multiple Tornado Charm - AWE-SOME! hehe). Had a cam chat with a guy in Germany (big cock and HOT body, seems like a cool lad indeed), shot another load watching him fingering his horny boyhole.

So, overall, just an average day in my life. Is it sex centered? Well, maybe a bit I have to admit haha. I did also try to burn some DVD's with my latest arty porn on it, using iDVD, to sell at the Berlin Porn Film Festival this autumn. I really don't get that program, so I failed miserably, hm. My neighbour came over and helped me though, and together we managed in the end. Oh, I almost forgot: I filmed a really horny group scene with hung muscle guy Massimo (I filmed with him in Newport earlier this year, too) for TIM. It was so fucking horny watching him take load after load in his muscle hole, hehe.

I met my sexy big cocked friend from Prague, Martin, whom I filmed with in earlier in the summer with - he was one of the tops, it was good to see him, if only briefly. Apart from that, I've been running around like mad man organizing another music video shoot on Saturday for awesome new group Mollyhause.

Oh, and you can see the trailer I edited for the Berlin Porn Film Festival on my webpage in the video section if you want, it also shows the previous years' I've done for them, so much fun one can have with arty porn of all sorts of styles and interest. Till next.

Hugs - Anton

Readers online comments:

I - Anton!! You are SO HOT mate!!!

    Ia - Hehe nah, I'm just normal, but thank u, Hugs a

WEEK XXIX

Losing my RELIGION; Baptized A CUMPIG

Hey, horny fuckers. This has been a crazy week, filming the music video as well as planning and doing test shoots for model agencies etc, so I thought I'd take this opportunity to write about some of the naughtier encounters I've had in the past - namely in and around religious buildings around the world. This one took place in a lovely, small, quiet Italian town in the north of Italy (it was either Modena or Ferrara; I'm so bad with names and never remember). I was on tour with my dance company at the time, performing Romeo and Juliet at the town's old theatre, an amazing building.

On my day off I wandered around the ancient city walls, which were large and grassed over, like the old medieval town it is. I was wearing tight red shorts that were rubbing against my crouch and it was a hot and sticky day, so of course I got a huge hard on almost poking out of the tiny shorts I was wearing.

I looked around - it was very quiet, just some old people walking slowly in front of me - and wondered where I could strip off or pull it out and have a wank. Then I spotted a few gravestones a bit to the right so I walked towards them. When I turned the corner, an amazing old Italian cemetery opened up in front of me, with large and small memorials and ancient crosses and statues all over the place. The statues were so beautiful, partly broken stone angels and cherubs decorating the mausoleums, some partly overgrown with wild flowers and green leaves, and some covered in spiderweb swaying in the light breeze.

I was like, "Awesome, a perfect desolate graveyard - exactly what I need!" I opened one of the half broken doors and went inside one of the old small mausoleums. A bunch of old, dusty plastic flowers was sticking out of a porcelain vase on the small altar next to a little timber crucifix. To the right of it were some fragile looking ceramic cups. I pulled down my pants after closing the door carefully behind me, and started to wank off slowly. Taking in every detail of the small chamber. After 10 minutes or so of enjoying my quiet wank in the hot weather, I noticed a mirror behind the altar and saw the reflection of a young man through the small side window of the chamber. I shrugged quickly and pulled up my pants. Too late - he had already seen me and was approaching. A thousand thoughts rushed through my brain. I decided to just pretend I didn't understand and ramble some gibberish in Swedish and run off (that had worked for me previously on numerous occasions being caught wanking in public I have to admit hehe...).

The door slowly opened and the young man entered. I was just about to start speaking when he hushed me with a finger on my lips and moved closer. I was so surprised, I just stood there. He was really hot, looked a bit like a straight, Italian gardener type of guy with his shirt half done up. Closing the door behind him, he than pushed me up against the altar and kissed me roughly. I responded by grabbing his firm bum and pulling him towards me. I was so surprised, but he started pulling on my pants and I helped him take them off. Then I undid his pants and went down on my knees, revealing his large sunkissed cock, juicy with excitement. I started sucking it and could taste his salty precum.

Pulling me up, he turned me around and started licking my bumhole till it was nice and wet. Then he pushed his cock straight up it. I yelped and jerked forward, not used to bottoming and especially not for such a big cock. The crucifix on the alter wobbled and fell to the ground, I didn't care. This was the first anonymous bareback cock I ever had, and I was loving every centimeter of it! He fucked me hard and built up to his climax. At the exact moment he pumped his load deep inside me, I shot my cum all over the crucifix on the floor in front of the altar. Three seconds later, I saw the shadow of an elderly woman in the mirror, as she walked by to lay some flowers on the grave next to the chamber we were in. Her gaze fixed on the ground while she walked slowly past, swaying slightly on her old legs. We both ducked down so fast, in total silence, still with our pants and shorts around our ankles, giggling quietly like little school boys. After the woman had passed, the young man kissed me goodbye and left. Still dripping cum out of my hole, I sat there for another hour, shaken yet excited.

I wonder what ever happened to him? Things we will never know, hm... Life is so strange, with all these random encounters and lives crossing our paths. It's truly miraculous. I do love life, and I love sex. Anyhow, if you want, you can check out on my webpage a little teaser I did, from a remix track for "Red Shoes" by Mollyhaus, featuring awesome model Igor Stepanov. Hope u like it, the main music video is still being edited.

Hugs – Anton

Readers online comments:

I - Seems more a dream than the reality bros! wakey wakey...
    Ia - What part is the dream? It's all true, I cross my
        heart and hope to die, Hugs a

II - The adrenaline rush you get from doing stuff like this is amazing. Public fucking with the chance of getting caught is always the best.
    IIa - Yeah I totally agree, so fucking hot, love the
        anonymity of it also hehe

III - OMG, HOT n' AMEN!
    IIIa - Amen indeed hehe

IV - I love anonymous sex and especially BAREBACK, partly because I only BB sex.

WEEK XXX

BERLIN CUTIES

Hey, all horny men (and boys) out there. This week has been sooooo awesome I really don't know where to begin, hehe. Me and Liam Cole ventured over to Berlin for the 7th Berlin Porn Film Festival, which screened a selection of new, old, experimental, arthouse, gay, lesbian, transgender, and straight porn in a big program over 5 days. It's been truly amazing, meeting film-makers from all over the world and seeing their varied work, learning so much about human sexuality and the way we express it. I have to admit I really love Berlin (especially as a temporary visitor) - its laid-back decadent and self-important, excelling even in its partly rundown areas and poorer quarters.

One night I went to Laboratory, an awesome HUGE sex club on two levels underneath the infamous club Berghain. Horny men in leather, sport shorts, fully nude, or partly clothed cruised around the dark corners of the club or hung around the bar with the rude bar staff. (They really were; I usually don't mind but I was a little surprised). I had ordered 1 coca-cola and got 2 bottles (special offer). But I wanted a glass to avoid too many bubbles in my nose, lol. Since the skinhead barman was already busy with others, I reached in a bit to get one from the rack of glasses inside the bar. He turned to me, grabbed my arm in a really tight squeeze, and said in a low, menacing voice, "If you reach over the bar again, I'll kill you!" I was totally taken aback and just nodded. A Swedish guy I'd just met in the cruising areas was really shaken by it too, though we later laughed about it, hehe. But still - Welcome to Berlin right? lol.

I later took the hot Swedish guy into a cubicle, where I licked his sexy, smooth hole till I shot a load over the floor. Later, in a different area, I rimmed his bum again while wanking him off and was rewarded with a big, juicy load in my mouth and beard. Hot! Before I met the Swedish guy, I sucked off two hot, veerrryy hung Argentinian guys in the smoking area and got to taste their huge loads too. The joy, hehe. It was getting colder in Berlin so we took a cab back home. I got back before Liam did, even though I also dropped the Swedish boy off first. The day after I was too knackered for any shags, but the one after that I met a really cute 20 year old boy. I told him I wanted to fuck him bareback and that I was HIV positive. He didn't object as he was poz too, but he said, "OK, you can fuck me bareback, but you will have to get me a pack of cigarettes." (That's like €5 - "I can manage that" I said, hehe.) He had an amazingly hot bum and when I started pounding him missionary, he looked up at me with his big Eastern European blue eyes and said, "Can I call you daddy?" It felt like my already massively big hard-on grew an inch or two, hehe, and I said casually, "Yeah, sure, boy. I'm your daddy!" while pounding him even harder haha... Love that role play!

On Sunday, when my head was spinning with too many films and I couldn't handle any more, I started watching one more film at the cinema but then I had to sneak out to the entrance hall to check my GayRomeo messages. I had a message from a very cute 18 year old boy, a little bit taller than me but nice and skinny. I asked him if I could fuck him bareback. He asked me what my status was and I said I was poZitive, and he said he had just found out a week ago that he was poZitive too.

He was a bit sad, so I asked if he wanted to meet to talk about it. He agreed and I went over. When he opened the door in his cute, little, oversized boxer-shorts, I got a hard on straight away; I couldn't help it. He must have felt the same - as before the door closed behind me, we were all over each other, kissing and making out. I rimmed his horny boyhole as he moaned with pleasure, enjoying the tongue getting deeper and deeper into him. Then I pushed my fat cock into him and, after ten minutes, we simultaneously shot our loads: mine in him and his all over his stomach, I licked it up eagerly.

We relaxed for a while, talking about our experiences. It turned out he was working as a rent boy and had been for some time. He just turned 18 in August. After that, I made my way back to the cinema and sneaked back into the screening (it was a long programme of short films), just in time for the final Q&A, where I was called up on the podium, puh, hectic day haha...

Oh, I almost forgot that me and Liam dropped into a sex club/shop in Schoeneberg to see what films they were selling. All the Treasure Island Media titles were well displayed in prominent positions ofcourse (awesome!). Because I was in some films for other studios, as well as being in most of Liam's films, I won in terms of which of us had the most films there (result!), haha.

Tomorrow we're going back to London. Thank god - my cock is overworked and needs some relaxing, hehe. See you then. Hugs and thanks to the wonderful Berlin team for organizing such an awesome festival. Oh btw, the audience seemed to enjoy my KUK 1 short film very much (I'll upload it shortly somewhere for you all to see it). The trailer was appreciated also, and I also managed to sell two of my large print photos in the exhibition, one of Paddy O'Brien, so I'm a very proud and happy man indeed.

Hugs, Anton
(P.S. Liam says hi.)

Readers online comments:

I - Excuse me , are you really HIV+ ?
    Ia - yeah sexy, hugs anton

II - So horny events, wish it was me!

WEEK   XXXI

SEXUAL LIBERATION

Hey, guys. My mum always told me about sexual liberation when I was young but I never quite knew what she meant. Later I came to understand she was talking about feminism and liberation from sexual stigmas and pressures in society, etc. For me, as a gay man in a big, multicultural city like London, true sexual liberation came much later and in a very bizarre way - in the way of this blog chronicles, actually.

There is something so emotionally gratifying (and horny, of course, hehe) about being able to have an output for all these naughty things I do and get myself into, and to share them with others without shame. Before I started writing these posts, I thought I lived in my own little world, tinkering along like normal but with this dark, bubbling, raw sexuality hidden under the surface, wanting to get out but somehow not managing to.

I've had sooo much amazing positive feedback from you guys out there reading my little random scribbles, and I'm very grateful and humbled by it all. You guys rock! Cruising toilets and random sex, etc. isn't all that bad after all. We all find our own ways around our sexuality, I think, and now I can proudly say to my mum that even I am sexually liberated, hehe. (I doubt it was like this, that she meant, but male sexuality is very different from female sexuality, I believe.) And I've decided to publish the Chronicles in book format (and you are reading it now hehe), both in e-book and paperback pocket size, hope you will like it too, no images though... haha.

Apart from these thoughts, this week has been very hectic. I got back from Berlin, and my hubby got back and started triple cleaning the flat (bless him, hehe). I've been editing the music video together with a friend. I had some amazing blowjobs in the cultural centre toilets, playing with some horny office boys, and of course tasting some real big man cock in the tube station toilets - love a good lunch load before my sandwich, hehe; daily protein shake, here we go.

Today I have a lunch date. A proper one ohh, wish me luck. We also spoke with an awesome Danish artist who wants us to do a music video for her next track release. Could be fun, hehe.

Till next time. Hugs – Anton

Readers online comments:

I - You make my mouth water Sir.....

II - Saw you recently walking around soho, wanted to say hello but was too shy ;) where do you go for sucking off in public toilets? Love to go down on a hot straight builder. ;)))
IIa - Hehe u Should have cum and said hello, I'm al-

ways happy to meet new horny guys hehe, and there is always a toilet available somewhere for a quick blow. Hugs a

III - Excuse me, are you really HIV+ ? thanks .
IIIa - Where does he mention being poz?
IIIb - Lets start from the beginning again... hehe.

Anton Dickson filmography:

1998 - Exposed - DVD (soft / hardcore safe)

2000 - The White Room - DVD (safe)
2002 - Ben Block - Vulcan Magazine
2002 - Chris Geary's - Web
2002 - Hard Games / Corolo - DVD (safe)
2002 - Ketchum - Andreas Johansson - Magazine
2002 - South London - Web
2002 - Steve Brewer - Web
2003 - Anabella - Web (straight / raw) (x 2 scenes)
2003 - BritBoys - Magazine
2003 - Casting Cards - Web
2003 - Lads UK - Web
2003 - LL Film - Web
2003 - Steve Brewer - Web
2003 - The Antton Harri Story Part 1 - The Beginning - DVD (safe
2004 - English Lads - Web (x 8 scenes)
2004 - Bad Puppy - Web
2004 - Daredevils - Web (straight)
2004 - Raspberry Reich - Bruce LaBruce - DVD feature (safe)
2004 - The Ultimate BoyParty - Freshwave - DVD (safe)
2004 - Young Vikings - Web

2005 - Boyz on the side, Love & Betrayal - Corolo (safe)
2005 - D & A - web unpublished
2005 - Emma & Anton - Web (straight / raw)
2005 - Lay your Bets - Freshwave - DVD (safe)
2005 - PhotoBoyz - Web
2005 - RandyBlue, Juicygoo - Web
2005 - Summer of the Masacre (non porn / horror)
2005 - The Second Cummin - FreshSX - DVD (safe)
2006 - In Bed with Spike - Freshwave - DVD (safe)
2007 - Television X - Web (straight)
2007 - The Agency - Screen Test 1 - Freshwave - DVD (safe)
2007 - What goes around... Freshwave - DVD (safe)
2008 - Boyzparty - Web
2008 - 2010 - Gogo Dancing (dancing in clubs - basically done this since I was 17 in Stockholm, Lille, Paris & London, including stripping & sex shows hehe always fun...)
2008 - Guyzstudioboyz - Web
2008 - Passion - Event / Show
2009 - Manimal - Chris Geary - Event / Web
2009 - Moby Dick - Art Video - Portugal (safe)
2009 - Paul DeDona - Web
2009 - Pounded (by Liam Cole) - Treasure Island Media (TIM) - DVD (raw)
2009 - Six of the Best - Freshwave - DVD (safe)
2009 - The Apprentice 1-3 - FreshSX - DVD (safe)
2009 - The Apprentice 3 - FreshSX - DVD (safe)

2009 - The Cock Inn - DVD (safe)

2010 - Fuck it's HUGE - DVD (safe)
2010 - 2013 - Fucking Lost - CAZZO - DVD (safe)
2010 - Full Tilt (by Liam Cole) - TIM - DVD (raw)
2010 - Cum on My Face Bitch! - FreshSX - DVD (safe)
2010 - Raw Hide - Cash Jasper - DVD (raw)
2011 - Anton Dickson by Haringman+ - Web
2011 - In the Flesh (by Liam Cole) - TIM - DVD (raw)
2011 - The Female Voyeur (by Petra Joy) - DVD (bisexual)
2012 - SLAMMED (by Liam Cole) - TIM - DVD (raw)
2012 - Bareback Backpackers - Millivres Prowler Ltd - DVD (raw)
2012 - Berlin Bare Butts - WURSTFILM - DVD (raw)
2012 - DarkRoom 1 - DarkAlley Media - DVD (raw)
2012 - Bareback Barebecue Party - Millivres Prowler Ltd - DVD (raw)
2012 - DarkRoom 2 - DarkAlley Media - DVD (raw)
2012 - Bareback Pool Party - Millivres Prowler Ltd - DVD (raw)
2013 - OVERLOAD (by Liam Cole) - TIM - DVD (raw)
2013 - DarkRoom 3 - DarkAlley Media - DVD (raw)
2013 - OUTLAWS (by Liam Cole) - TIM - DVD (raw)

External links:

@AntonDicksonX
www.anton-dickson.tumblr.com
www.treasureislandblog.com/anton-dickson
www.facebook.com/anton.dickson.58
www.xtube.com/community/profile.php?user=anton-dickson
www.blurb.com/user/atelier-az
www.atelier-az.org

ISBN 978-91-87617-00-3

the END

VOLUME I

...volume II to follow

hugs anton